M000220805

A BEWITCHED LAND

Ireland's witches, wise women and warlocks

Bob Curran is an educational psychologist at the University of Ulster, Coleraine. He also works extensively in community education and with adults in return-to-education schemes. His community-based approach links him with the history and folklore of many areas all over Ireland. His interests are broad-ranging but are focused especially on history and story. He has written several books, including *The Field Guide to Irish Fairies*, *The Wolfhound Guide to the Shamrock*, *Creatures of Celtic Myth*, *The Truth about the Leprechaun* and *A Haunted Land: Ireland's Ghosts*.

A Bewitched Land

IRELAND'S WITCHES

Bob Curran

THE O'BRIEN PRESS
DUBLIN

First published 2005 by The O'Brien Press Ltd,
20 Victoria Road, Dublin 6, Ireland.
Tel: +353 1 4923333; Fax: +353 1 4922777
E-mail: books@obrien.ie
Website: www.obrien.ie

ISBN: 0-86278-899-4

Text © copyright Bob Curran 2005
Copyright for typesetting, layout, editing, design
© The O'Brien Press Ltd

All rights reserved. No part of this publication may be reproduced
or utilised in any form or by any means, electronic or mechanical,
including photocopying, recording or in any information storage
and retrieval system, without permission in writing
from the publisher.

Every effort has been made to trace holders of copyright material
used in this book, but if any infringement of copyright has inadvertently
occurred the publishers ask the copyright holders to contact them immediately.

British Library Cataloguing-in-Publication Data
A catalogue record for this title is available from the British Library

1 2 3 4 5 6 7 8 9 10

05 06 07 08 09

Layout and design: The O'Brien Press Ltd
Printing: Nørhaven Paperback A/S

CONTENTS

Introduction

'To the Catholics their fairies and the Protestants their witches' ran an old saying in the north of Ireland at one time. This would, on the face of it, suggest that Ireland was fairly rife with instances of witchcraft and that it occurred in largely Protestant areas of the country. This is not wholly true. In fact, according to the records, there appear to have been very few formal cases of witchcraft in Ireland. Compared with areas such as Essex in England, the recorded material regarding witchcraft trials is very scarce indeed.

This, of course, does not mean that there was no witchcraft in Ireland. It could mean one of two things – first, that evidence concerning instances of witchcraft and trials of alleged witches has been lost or (more likely) that few formal instances of witchcraft were ever brought to trial in Ireland. Witchcraft certainly existed throughout the country but, one suspects, it was regarded quite differently than it was in England or Scotland.

Under the laws of both Church and State, witchcraft was viewed in different ways, depending upon the country concerned. In England, for example, it was viewed as *maleficium* (evil doing), a crime against society, and was therefore treated as a felony under the civil law. Historians such as Keith Thomas in his seminal book on English witchcraft, *Religion and the Decline of Magic,* and Alan MacFarlane in his *Witchcraft in Tudor and Stuart England* have shown how English witchcraft was firmly rooted in social disputes, individual envy, communal injustices and interpersonal dislike, coupled with a changing social ethos. The idea of witchcraft seemed to spring from spite and hatred of one's neighbours — an ill-wishing, as it were, against those who were socially better or socially different — and English law reflected such thinking: few alleged English witches were burned, all were hanged, the traditional punishment for a felony.

On the Continent and in Scotland, however, the position was very different. Here, the notion of witchcraft was fundamentally religious and involved the complicity of Satan, the Evil One, the Enemy of All Mankind. In return for earthly powers, witches were considered to have thrown in their lot with diabolical forces — usually at the expense of their immortal souls — and had turned upon the servants and followers of Christ. In doing so, they had completely renounced Christ's salvation and had rejected His love. They were beyond help and would ultimately burn in the fires of Hell. Under Continental law, then, witchcraft was heresy — an offence against both the laws of Man and the laws of God — and those who practised it were to be burned. The

Continental view made its way to Scotland with Protestant clerics and Reformers such as George Wishart and John Knox around the end of the 1500s. Scotland became one of the very few parts of the British Isles where old women were placed on blazing tar barrels or burnt at the stake in town and village squares. Ireland, it would appear, was curiously oblivious to all this and stood apart from the witch-persecutions which sporadically afflicted its neighbours. Or did it?

What particular form of behaviour constituted witchcraft? What set the alleged witch apart from his or her community? And did this sort of behaviour appear in Ireland? As with England and Scotland, the answer lay in the context of local community relations.

There is some evidence to suggest that both versions of the witch-belief – English and Continental – prevailed in Ireland as well. In many parts of the countryside there were people (mainly women) who displayed both skills and knowledge which were considered to be beyond the capabilities of ordinary mortals. Such people may have had a knowledge of herblore, a way with livestock or a highly intuitive ability to foretell the future. However, although these 'powers' were usually acknowledged as being supernatural, such people were not necessarily deemed to be witches – rather they were referred to as 'wise women' or 'fairy doctors' by their community. Indeed, they were regarded as integral members of society – often acting as doctors and midwives in areas where no formal medicine existed or as 'advisors' in the years before a communal counselling service came into being. Nevertheless, it was generally agreed that because of their alleged powers, it was unwise to cross them and that some misfortune would ensue if the wise woman or fairy doctor 'took against' a person. Farmers knew that if they spoke rudely to some old woman living alone on the edge of their property or if they refused her charity, their crops could fail, their cattle might fall ill, or worse – a member of their family might die. Such people were to be treated with respect.

In many cases, a reputation like this was sometimes the only way in which the old or the particularly vulnerable could obtain any sort of status in their communities. In a chauvinistic rural society, a widow woman, perhaps with no man to provide for her or to look after her, was especially susceptible to hardship. However, if the other members of the community feared her, they would treat her with caution and provide for her when she asked. Thus, as elsewhere, vulnerable people encouraged such beliefs about themselves by deliberately adopting and developing eccentric and independent ways. For women this was especially easy. Many male-dominated communities demanded certain behaviour patterns from the women in their midst. These were enforced by another male-dominated organisation – the Church. Therefore, it was not hard for independent women to outrage the forces of social morality by behaving in non-acceptable ways. And the way in which some women did this was to behave like a man — thus some women smoked, drank to excess and played cards, just like their male counterparts. Such behaviour drew attention to them and through it they acquired a reputation. If this behaviour was linked to alleged supernatural powers, then the person in question was deemed to be a 'wise woman' or in some other cases 'touched by the fairies'. From their pulpits, the clergy denounced such people — women especially — as being outside the Church and 'in dire need of salvation'.

It was a small step in certain localities from such denunciations of outlandish behaviour towards what might be described as a more 'Continental' viewpoint. Such women were not only flouting the Church and its teachings, they were deliberately courting the Devil and his minions. The north of Ireland, in particular, had been strongly influenced by Calvinistic Protestant doctrines introduced by Scottish settlers during the Ulster Plantation. In areas steeped in such a strict religious view, the Devil was everywhere, seeking through his agents to lead God's people astray or to do them harm. What better way to do so than to enlist the help of such eccentric women and mould them for his own purposes by offering them earthly power and status? Thus the fiercely independent man or woman with his or her 'arcane' knowledge and odd ways became an instrument of the Evil One and those who consulted them were placing their immortal souls in terrible danger. At least, so ran

Church teaching. Nevertheless, in many instances, the so-called witches continued to enjoy both status and reputation in their specific communities. Those who were forbidden by the authorities to consult them often did so secretly, adding to the air of sinister mystery which surrounded these local practitioners. And the Church continued to fume and fulminate against them.

Occasionally such accusations *did* spill over into formal trials. These occurred particularly in areas of Ireland that had become heavily Anglicised – places like Youghal in County Cork or Carrickfergus in County Antrim – and may have reflected a more 'English' view of the matter. The case of Florence Newton, for example, with its curses and witchfinders, reflects many of the characteristics of English witchcraft cases recorded in places such as Essex. But there were Continental influences in some of the trials too, especially in areas that had been settled by those espousing religious doctrines derived from Continental Calvinism, most notably the Presbyterians of Ulster. It is interesting to note that at least one witchcraft trial in the north of Ireland – the Islandmagee case in the early eighteenth century – bears all the hallmarks of the Salem experience in 1692, which occurred in a New England community heavily influenced by Calvinist beliefs.

In the rural Irish countryside, however, the wise women and fairy doctors continued to ply their trade undeterred. Local figures such as Biddy Early in Clare and Moll Anthony in Kildare continued to give out cures, love potions and curses, just as they'd always done and although a number of Witchcraft Acts were passed in England, supposedly to limit the influence of such practitioners, in rural Ireland they seem to have had little effect. Moreover, many of these alleged 'witches' were steadily acquiring a reputation far beyond their own localities. Biddy Early, the famous 'wise woman of Clare', for example, was well-known even as far away as the Isle of Man and people were prepared to travel from places like Douglas to her cottage at Kilbarron to consult her. And of course, as the reputation of these people grew, so did the legends and stories about them, sometimes to wild and improbable heights — Biddy Early was said to have a magic bottle in which she could foresee the future, spy on her neighbours or pin-point the location of lost objects, whilst Maurice Griffin, a legendary 'fairy doctor' of Kerry, was supposed to have received his powers by drinking milk from a cow which had been overwhelmed by a supernatural cloud. In many cases, the individuals concerned supported these fables as it added to their status as practitioners of the dark and magical arts.

A formal belief in witchcraft by the authorities seems to have declined around the beginning of the eighteenth century, mirroring developments in England where witchcraft trials began to die out at around this time. Informally, however, 'wise women and fairy men' continued to practise in rural areas right up until the twentieth century and some may still practise in the remoter regions of the countryside even today. Indeed, the last instance of alleged witchcraft in which the law was involved occurred in Ballyvadlea, County Tipperary, as recently as 1895. This case is discussed in the fourth chapter of the book.

The figure of the Irish witch, then, is a complicated one, comprising a number of functions (midwife, healer, mischief worker) and a number of strands of belief (Celtic, English, Continental). In many instances it is extremely difficult to untangle these in order to get a clear picture of what was really going on. The overlap between traditional notions of witchcraft as found in Britain and on the Continent and the widespread Irish vernacular belief in fairies, in particular, resulted in a distinctively Irish 'take' on witchcraft and associated supernatural matters.

This book sets out to tell the story of Irish witchcraft in all its variety. It has been divided into three sections. The first section examines the history of witchcraft trials in Ireland (the last chapter in this section, on Bridget Cleary, having a slightly different emphasis in that the people brought to trial were not accused of witchcraft as such but rather of murdering a woman they considered to be a changeling). The second section focuses on the stories surrounding wise women and 'hedge witches', and includes a chapter on the most celebrated of these figures, Biddy Early. The third and final section relates folk tales and anecdotes concerning lesser known Irish witches and other sinister individuals such as 'The Wizard Earl' of Lough Gur, 'The Black Hag' of Shanagolden in

Limerick and the Ulster warlock Alexander Colville, who is reputed to have sold his soul to the Devil.

In outlining the prevalent perceptions which determined belief in witchcraft in this country and in presenting a picture of Irish witchcraft that is both as rich and vivid as the folklore that surrounds the subject, this book will hopefully tell us something about ourselves — our beliefs and fears and the way in which we see the world.

Witchcraft Trials in Ireland

Dame Alice Kyteler

THE KILKENNY SORCERESS (1324)

Although traditionally witches were hanged throughout the British Isles (with the exception of Scotland), the first actual witch *burning* took place in Ireland. And, just to confuse matters even further, it was not the alleged witch who was burnt but rather her servant. The year was 1324 and the place was the then wealthy town of Kilkenny.

Of course the burning predates any formal witchcraft statute in the country and therefore relies on ecclesiastical law (which treated witchcraft as heresy) rather than English common law (which treated it as a felony). Still, the case was characterised by the same petty jealousies and personal spites which were symptomatic of later, English trials. There was also the added dimension of a struggle for power between the religious and secular authorities, in a wealthy merchant town and in a country that was going through a period of transition and consolidation.

Kilkenny was a thriving and prosperous town. It had grown from a settlement around a monastery founded by St Canice (c.AD514-598/600) who had been reputedly born in the Roe

Valley in County Derry but had travelled south bringing the Gospel with him and founding churches and religious houses. In the twelfth and thirteenth centuries, the town was a Norman one, having received its first Charter in 1208, granted by William the Marshal, the Earl of Pembroke, and for a long time it was the centre of important decisions for the area and for most of Ireland as well. It was from here that the incoming English planters issued statutes that governed many of their relationships with the native Irish. And the monastic tradition still seems to have been very strong in the area – Kilkenny was certainly a base for the important Diocese of Ossory. As Kilkenny began to develop as a trading town, with many artisans setting up business there, the secular and the religious authorities, both regulating various aspects of everyday life, must have come into conflict.

The underlying tensions between Church and State came to something of a head with the accusations of witchcraft that appeared in the town early in the fourteenth century and which centred around a prominent woman in the community.

Although she has sometimes been portrayed as an old, shrivelled hag, Dame Alice Kyteler (or Kettle) was probably nothing of the kind. Indeed, she was in all likelihood quite a handsome woman, as evidenced by the fact that she was married four times, on each occasion to prominent Norman noblemen. Her first husband, William Outlawe, was a town banker, by whom she bore a son, also called William. This husband seems to have died rather mysteriously and very soon afterwards Dame Alice got married again — this time to the wealthy Adam de Blund of Callan, to whom she seems to have borne more children. Once again, he died quickly and mysteriously, leaving Dame Alice free to take a third husband, Richard de Valle. Some time after he, too, took sick and died and following his demise Dame Alice began to look around for another husband. This time it was Sir John le Poer, a wealthy landowner. By now, the sequential deaths of Dame Alice's unfortunate husbands were becoming a source of some scandal in Kilkenny and a number of questions were being asked. Even before she had married, Alice seems to have been a reasonably prosperous woman but the estates of three husbands had enriched her considerably.

It was not long before Dame Alice's fourth husband began to show signs of illness. He appears to have become weak and sickly and, fearing he was dying, resolved to change his will in order to provide for his widow. Included in this settlement, it appears, was a provision for Dame Alice's eldest and allegedly favourite son, William Outlawe. Sir John had been married before and had a family from his previous marriage who were not at all pleased at being ousted from their inheritance by this now-suspicious lady and her son. They approached a leading churchman, Richard de Ledrede, an English-born Franciscan friar who was Bishop of Ossory, and laid a charge in front of him that something was not right and that their stepmother had somehow 'bewitched' their father and had made him 'take leave of his senses'. It was also hinted that Dame Alice might have poisoned her three previous husbands. In medieval Ireland (as in England) the term 'poisoner' was usually synonymous with 'witch', since both implied an arcane knowledge of herbs and philtres. De Ledrede promised that he would investigate.

On a diocesan visit to Kilkenny in 1324, he convened a Court of Inquisition, which comprised five knights and several nobles, to examine the facts of the case. It seems, according to some sources, that de Ledrede was determined to establish the rule of the Church in an increasingly wealthy but secularised Kilkenny and that he was obsessed with the occult and with witchcraft. The Kyteler case allowed him to give vent to both of these obsessions.

After much deliberation, presumably guided by the bishop, the Inquisition reached a somewhat startling conclusion. There was, it declared, a coven or band of 'heretical sorcerers' actively operating in the town of Kilkenny, the head of whom was Dame Alice herself. No doubt inspired by de Ledrede, the Inquisition laid the following charges against them.

> That they had denied the faith of Christ absolutely, for a year or a month, according to the value or importance of the object which they desired to gain through sorcery. During all that period they believed in none of the doctrines of the Church and they did not adore the Body of Christ, nor did they enter a sacred building or hear the Mass or receive or make use of the Sacraments.

That they offered sacrifices to demons of living animals, which they dismembered and then scattered at the crossroads in honour of a certain spirit 'of low rank' which was named as Robin, Son of Art (or Artisson).

That they had sought, by their sorcery, advice, encouragement and responses from demons.

That they had blasphemously imitated the power of the Church by imposing, by the light of three tallow candles, a sentence of excommunication against their own husbands from the soles of their feet to the crowns of their heads, specifically naming each part of the body and then concluding the 'service' by extinguishing the candles and by crying *'Fi! Fi! Fi! Amen'*.

That in order to arouse feelings of love or hatred, or to inflict death or disease upon the bodies of the faithful, they made use of powders, unguents, ointments and candles of fat which were made up as follows. They took the entrails of cocks sacrificed to demons, 'certain horrible worms', various unspecified herbs, dead men's nails, the hair, brains and shreds of the cerements of boys who were buried unbaptised, with other abominations, all of which they cooked with various incantations, over a fire of oak logs in a vessel made out of the skull of a decapitated thief.

The children of Dame Alice's four husbands had accused her of having harmed their fathers by sorcery and poison and of having brought, by the use of potions and powders, John le Poer to a state whereby he had become terribly emaciated, his nails had dropped off and there was no hair left on his body. He had at this stage been warned of Dame Alice's magic by a maidservant and had given into the hands of the bishop via certain priests, a sackful of 'horrible and detestable things'. Dame Alice was further accused of muddling her husbands' minds by sorcery so that they bequeathed all their wealth to her favourite son, William Outlawe.

It was also alleged that the male demon known as Robin, Son of Art, or Artisson, was Dame Alice's incubus and that he had had carnal knowledge of her, and furthermore that she had admitted that it was from him that she received her wealth. This minor demon was said to have made frequent and often violent appearances in various forms, sometimes as a cat, sometimes as a fierce and hairy black dog, and sometimes in the guise of a Negro ('Æthiops') accompanied by two other devils that were usually larger and taller than he, one of whom carried an iron rod. These demons, it was said, were conjured up by sacrificing fowls (nine red cocks) and the offering of peacocks' eyes.

Several worthy people of Kilkenny, no doubt with the guidance of de Ledrede, stated that they had seen Dame Alice sweeping the streets of the town with a long broom between the hours of sunset and sunrise. As she raked all the muck and filth from the street, these witnesses claimed that they heard her repeat the following incantation:

'To the house of William my sonne
Hie all the wealth of Kilkennie towne'.

The accusations reflect the paranoia of the Continental notions of witchcraft – the coven (gathering) of witches meeting to do harm to their community; sacrifices to Satan of animals; the ghastly ingredients of their unguents and candles; the suggestion that Dame Alice had sexual intercourse with a male demon; the suggestion that the sorcerers mocked the rituals of the Christian Mass with their blasphemies – all of these were the stock-in-trade of the early Continental Christian writers on witchcraft. They also probably reflected the mind of de Ledrede himself.

As soon as the Inquisition reached its conclusions, Bishop de Ledrede immediately wrote to the Prior of Kilmainham and Chancellor of Ireland, Roger Outlawe, requesting that a number of persons, including Dame Alice and her son, be arrested on charges of witchcraft. As his surname suggests, Roger Outlawe was a close relative of Dame Alice's first husband and therefore also of her son William.

Outraged by the accusations against him, William Outlawe formed a group of influential figures to resist the bishop's demands. Among these was Sir Arnold le Poer who was probably a kinsman of Dame Alice's fourth husband and also Seneschal of Kilkenny. As one of the leading administrators and public figures of the town, his inclusion in the opposition to de Ledrede was significant.

Replying to the bishop, Chancellor Outlawe pointed out that an arrest warrant could not be issued until the accused had been formally excommunicated by the Church for forty days. At the same time, Sir Arnold wrote to de Ledrede asking him to withdraw the case or else ignore or forget about it. This was to mark the start of a struggle between the two men — reflecting the struggle between the secular and religious powers for control of Kilkenny.

Incensed by the seneschal's suggestion that he should 'ignore' such a grave religious matter as witchcraft and stung by the chancellor's indifference, de Ledrede took matters into his own hands and summonsed the Dame, who was then residing with her son William within the Kilkenny boundary, to appear before him and to give an account of herself. Not surprisingly, Dame Alice chose to ignore the summons and fled to relatives in England, well beyond de Ledrede's reach, whereupon the bishop promptly excommunicated her. However her son, William Outlawe, remained in Kilkenny and it was towards him that a frustrated de Ledrede now turned his attention. He cited William for heresy, instructing him to appear before him within seventeen days.

At this, William and Sir Arnold came to the Priory of Kells where de Ledrede was holding a Visitation and Sir Arnold demanded, as seneschal, that he should proceed no further with the allegations. Finding any pleading with the bishop fruitless, the seneschal threatened the bishop with arrest. Going back to Kilkenny, he made good this threat and, as Bishop de Ledrede left Kells, he was met by the Sheriff of the area and Bailiff of the Cantred of Overk, Stephen le Poer, accompanied by a party of armed men who immediately arrested him on the seneschal's orders. He was taken back to Kilkenny under armed guard and thrown into the jail.

* * *

Not surprisingly, the arrest and imprisonment caused great interest and controversy all around Kilkenny and a number of churchmen flocked to the jail to offer support to the bishop. In his official status, the bishop placed an interdict on Kilkenny, which meant that none of the leading figures of the town – those who had been involved in de Ledrede's arrest – could receive the Sacrament. However, it also meant that no Mass could be said in the town until the interdict was lifted. De Ledrede himself made a great show of receiving the sacraments of the Church himself and a Dominican friar preached a sermon in front of Kilkenny jail, taking as his text *Blessed are they which are persecuted.* Fearing a popular revolt in the town, William Outlawe urged Sir Arnold to keep the bishop under closer restraint and this the seneschal did for a time, but he later nervously revoked his instruction, allowing de Ledrede to have companions with him, both day and night, and to receive visitors when he wished. He was also allowed to have servants and to receive the Sacrament, if and when he desired. The bishop was now becoming something of a martyr figure.

Seventeen days passed and de Ledrede remained in custody. By now the seventeen days which he had given William Outlawe to appear before him had passed. Sir Arnold, feeling that he had achieved what he had set out to do, sent his uncle, Miler le Poer, the Bishop of Leighlin, together with the Sheriff of Kilkenny to set the prisoner free. Still fearing a riot, Miler le Poer asked de Ledrede to leave quietly and without fuss, hopefully by the back door of the jail, but de Ledrede, now full of pious indignation, refused. He would not sneak out, he declared, like some common felon, he would leave like the bishop that he was. Attired in his full pontificals and accompanied by a great throng of clergy and townspeople, he made his way from the jail to St Canice's Cathedral in the town to give thanks to God for his release. At the doors of the church, he demanded that William Outlawe present himself before him to answer a charge of witchcraft. It seemed that William had no other option but to comply.

The day before he was due to appear, however, the bizarre story took another twist. Bishop de Ledrede himself was cited to appear before an ecclesiastical court in Dublin to answer a charge of having unlawfully placed an interdict on the town of Kilkenny. At the bottom of this, probably, lay manoeuvrings by Sir Arnold and his associates but this could not be proved. The bishop pleaded that he could not attend, as he would have to travel to Dublin through lands which were held by Sir Arnold and that he feared for his life. The seneschal, however, seized the opportunity to convene a court himself to try the bishop for his unlawful conduct.

The seneschal's court was held at Easter 1324 (de Ledrede had been arrested during Lent) and although the bishop turned up for it, he was denied entrance. Not to be deterred, however, he forced his way into the courtroom, fully robed and carrying the Sacrament in a golden vase. As it was Easter, he elevated the Host and amidst the prayers and hymns of his followers, he demanded that the seneschal, the bailiffs and the court give him a fair hearing. This was eventually granted, although allegedly with an ill will from Sir Arnold.

The court then descended into an unedifying spectacle that did neither the Church nor the civil authorities any credit. In fact, it degenerated into a shouting match with one side trying to outdo the other in trading insults. Sir Arnold, for example, referred to the bishop as 'that vile, rustic, interloping monk with dirty hands' and refused to hear anything that de Ledrede said or to grant him any aid whilst in court. The proceedings were adjourned before violence broke out.

* * *

In the interim, Dame Alice Kyteler herself, who seems to have taken a peripheral role in these events, had not been idle. She had returned from England to Dublin, where she lobbied the archbishop to convene a court against de Ledrede for having unlawfully excommunicated her on an unproven charge of witchcraft. De Ledrede presented himself to the archbishop's court and was found to have acted 'in error' and was forced to lift the excommunication. However, after hearing of the almost comical proceedings in Kilkenny, the archbishop had stern words for Sir Arnold le Poer. The seneschal was humbled and was forced to apologise to the bishop for the wrongs that he had done him. In the presence of the assembled prelates, he was obliged to offer de Ledrede the kiss of peace, which the other (somewhat unwillingly) accepted.

Bishop de Ledrede, however, was not a man to give up easily. Returning from Dublin to Kilkenny, he immediately wrote to the chancellor, Roger Outlawe, directing that he arrest Dame Alice (still in Dublin), and also to the Vicar General of the Archbishop of Dublin, demanding that she be returned to Kilkenny to answer the witchcraft charges. Dame Alice seems to have got wind of these letters and once again made her escape to England, this time never to return. Behind her, however, the witchcraft allegations persisted.

On de Ledrede's orders, several of her alleged confederates were arrested as witches and thrown into prison. A good number of them came from a relatively poor or 'middling sort' of background and, as such, offered little resistance. Their names were: Robert of Bristol, a clerk; Petronilla of Meath, who had been a personal servant to Dame Alice, and her daughter Sarah; John, Ellen and Syssok Galrussyn; Annota Lange, Eva de Brownestown, William Payne de Boly and Alice, the wife of Henry Faber.

Returning from a visit to Dublin, the bishop went straight to Kilkenny prison and interviewed all the prisoners who admitted their guilt straightaway, confessing their blasphemous crimes and mentioning others, which had not been specified. Dame Alice, they all declared, had been 'the mother and mistress of them all'. There is little doubt that all of them were terrified and would readily have admitted to anything, and no doubt de Ledrede 'guided' all their confessions. Armed with this 'evidence', the bishop then wrote to Roger Outlawe, as Chancellor of Ireland, requesting that all the witches be lodged in jail pending their trial. This may have included William Outlawe, Dame Alice's son. The chancellor refused to issue the necessary warrant, probably on the unstated grounds that William was a relative and a close friend. Bishop de Ledrede then obtained it through the Justiciary of Ireland, who consented to deal with the case when he came to Kilkenny. Dame Alice's son, however, was not named.

Before the Justiciary's arrival, the bishop requested that William Outlawe appear before him at St Mary's Church to answer charges of witchcraft. William certainly appeared there but he was accompanied by a band of men, all armed to the teeth. Unperturbed by this show of force, Bishop de Ledrede formally denounced him as a witch and a heretic and accused him of favouring, receiving and defending heretics, as well as of usury, perjury, adultery, clericide and a number of other crimes and blasphemies. In all, the bishop accused him of thirty-four crimes against the laws of man and of God, to which he was not permitted to respond until the Justiciary had arrived in Kilkenny. When the lawman reached the town, he was accompanied by Chancellor Outlawe and the Irish Treasurer, Walter de Islep, as well as the King's Council and several other notable legal men. In front of this august company, de Ledrede recited a list of charges against Dame Alice and with the common consent of all those lawyers present, she was declared to be a sorceress and a heretic. Emboldened, de Ledrede demanded that she now should be handed over to the secular arm for trial wherever she resided (this was not done) and that her goods and chattels should be confiscated (this apparently was done on 2 July 1324). On the same day, de Ledrede lit a great fire in the central market square of the town and with great ceremony burned a sackful of materials that were believed to contain ointments, powders, philtres, dead men's fingernails, worms, spiders, the fat of murdered infants and 'other abominations'. These were the items which he had received from Dame Alice's fourth husband, John le Poer, after the latter had ransacked her house. The bishop declared that the Dame also had a staff on which she 'ambled and galloped through thick and thinne' but he had not been able to locate its whereabouts.

Triumphant and seemingly filled with a holy zeal, de Ledrede now called upon William Outlawe to appear before him on his knees to show abject contrition for his former sins. At first Outlawe refused and in this he was backed by the chancellor and the treasurer, but so great was de Ledrede's following in the town that he was finally compelled to do so. By way of a penance, the bishop ordered that he attend at least three Masses every day for a year; that he had to feed a certain number of the poor and that he had to repair the roof of the chancel of St Canice's Cathedral from the belfry eastward and to reroof the Chapel of the Blessed Virgin, all at his own expense. William agreed to do all of this but soon neglected his obligations and was promptly thrown into prison.

Having dealt satisfactorily with Dame Alice and her son, Bishop de Ledrede turned his attention to her alleged accomplices. How he dealt with them, and their eventual fate, is unknown — except in one instance. The unfortunate Petronilla of Meath, who had been Dame Alice's close servant, was now made a scapegoat for her absent mistress. It was against her that the bishop ordered his most stringent torture — perhaps because she had also been friendly with Dame Alice. She was flogged a number of times and terrible tortures were used to extract a confession from her. In the face of such pain, she made frequent admissions of diabolical guilt. She had, she confessed, denied her faith and had sacrificed to specific demons, most notably Robin, Son of Art, and through his magic, she had caused certain women whom she knew (and probably disliked) to appear as if they had goat's horns on their foreheads. Not surprisingly, she confirmed de Ledrede's allegations that the Dame had frequently consulted with demons of the most hideous sort and stated that although she (Petronilla) was a sorceress and extremely able in the Black Arts, she was nothing as compared to Dame Alice herself, from whom she had learned all her diabolical knowledge. Indeed, the unfortunate servant avowed, there were fewer magicians in all the world more capable in evil ways than the Dame. Petronilla also, unsurprisingly, declared that William Outlawe deserved death as much as she did, for he had observed and, on occasion, taken part in the worship of demons. For a year and a day he had further worn the Devil's Girdle (a magical belt) about his body to give him secular power.

Acting on information given to them by the tortured victims, de Ledrede's followers again searched Dame Alice's house where they found, hidden away, the greasy staff by means of which she 'ambled and galloped through thick and thinne where and in what manner she listed', a pipe of infernal ointment and a Sacramental Wafer which had the Devil's name stamped on it instead of that of Jesus Christ. This was the final proof of all their guilt. On the orders of Bishop de Ledrede, Petronilla was condemned to be burnt alive and the sentence was carried out 'with all due solemnity' in Kilkenny on Sunday, 3 November 1324.

The execution of the unfortunate Petronilla is the only record of a burning that we have in the case. There is no evidence of what happened to her co-accused, though it is highly possible that a number of them were burned as well. Indeed, there were suggestions that Petronilla's execution was the beginning rather than the end of the affair. An unnamed writer of the time who chronicled these events states: 'With regard to the other heretics and sorcerers who belonged to the pestilential society of Robin, son of Art, the order of law being preserved, some of them were publicly burnt to death; others, confessing their crimes in the presence of all the people, in an upper garment, were marked back and front with a cross after they had abjured their heresy, as is the custom; others were solemnly whipped through the town and the market-place; others were banished from the city and diocese; others who evaded the jurisdiction of the Church were excommunicated, while others again fled in fear and were never heard of after. And thus, by the authority of Holy Mother Church, and by the special grace of God, that most foul brood was scattered and destroyed.'

* * *

Bishop de Ledrede, however, was still not completely satisfied. Arnold le Poer, who had made life difficult for him, had thrown him into prison and slandered him at the Easter court, was next to be attacked. The bishop had him excommunicated and committed as a prisoner to Dublin Castle. Le Poer had the sympathy of many prominent people including Roger Outlawe, the chancellor. Outlawe, who was later to be appointed Justiciary of Ireland in 1328, showed the seneschal great kindness and treated him with leniency. This, of course, enraged de Ledrede and he actually accused the chancellor of heresy and of 'harbouring sorcerers'. The fires of the witchcraft scandal had clearly not died down in the bishop's breast. There was of course, no basis for de Ledrede's frenzied allegations and a subsequent committee of venerable clerics found Outlawe innocent of the charges, in return for which he prepared them all a sumptuous banquet, much to the bishop's displeasure. Sir Arnold le Poer was not so fortunate. He died whilst still in prison in 1331 and because he was still under excommunication, his body lay unburied for a long time. It seemed that the bishop had won most of his battles but there was still one final twist to be played out.

Shortly after Sir Arnold's death, Bishop de Ledrede found *himself* accused of heresy by a leading churchman, Alexander de Bicknor. The bishop immediately appealed to the Holy See and set out for Rome to declare his innocence. He was to be away from his diocese for quite some time and suffered many hardships on his journey. Whilst he was gone, the Crown seized his temporal lands, forcing him to return. He managed to regain his property in 1339 but ten years later a further charge of heresy against him was made directly to the English king, Edward III, and his lands were confiscated yet again. He was also threatened by a number of measures which might have even affected his bishopric. By 1356, however, some kind of peace had been restored and he looked reasonably secure once more. Nevertheless, he had not recovered all his lands.

Although the storm generated by the Kyteler case had more or less blown over, de Ledrede was still not a happy man. His long and turbulent episcopate ended with his death in 1360. He was buried in the chancel of St Canice's Cathedral on the north side of the high altar. With his death, the first recorded case of Irish witchcraft and the ill feeling that it had generated and which had rumbled on for decades finally came to an end.

Did Dame Alice actually practise the things of which she was accused? Whether or not her alleged spells and rituals were successful, did she actually *believe* herself to be an instrument of Satan and so inspire those who were accused with her? These events happened so many centuries ago that it is impossible for us to know the exact truth of the circumstances. Richard de Ledrede clearly pursued her and her accomplices with the full weight of ecclesiastical law. Certainly, the bishop seems to have been a somewhat unsympathetic character — single-minded, overbearing and dictatorial, utterly convinced of the supremacy of the laws of the Church, which he represented, over those of the State.

And yet, Richard de Ledrede may have been no more than a churchman who was representative of his time. A number of commentators have pointed out that the appointment of de Ledrede to the See of Ossory coincided with the elevation of the paranoid John XXII to the Papacy. The French Pope (1316-1334) had, perhaps justifiably, an inordinate fear of the political intrigues that were besetting the Papacy, and believed that witchcraft was being used as an instrument against him. Consequently, from around 1320 onwards, in a series of Papal Bulls, he anathematised sorcery and authorised strenuous persecutions of suspected witches by churchmen as part of their mission. Witchcraft had now been formally identified by the Holy Father as a cancer blighting society and the merest hint of it must be rooted out.

But probably the real basis for the accusations against Dame Alice was no more than the petty spites and jealousies of disgruntled stepchildren who believed that she had cheated them out of their rightful inheritance. Family hatreds and quarrels must have boiled over as William Outlawe assumed the wealth and property which others felt should have been rightfully theirs. In such circumstances, the accusation of witchcraft provided a ready and easy weapon. The bishop's own character simply stirred the embers of discontent into a fire of alleged heresy.

The Kyteler case is still remembered, especially around Kilkenny. Today there is even a public house in the town which bears the name The Kyteler Inn and tourist companies sometimes include Kilkenny on their routes as a 'witch town', and as the site of one of the earliest witch-burnings. Even in the twenty-first century, almost eight hundred years after the awful events, the Dame can still cast a long shadow.

Florence Newton

THE WITCH OF YOUGHAL (1661)

Although similarities can be traced between English and Irish witchcraft allegations, there are also a number of differences. As writers and historians like Keith Thomas and Alan MacFarlane have shown, citing studies in Essex, an area where witchcraft trial records are still largely extant, much English 'witchcraft' was based in tightly-knit, often rural communities (similar to those that existed throughout Ireland), and was in many cases a response to the needs, preoccupations and aspirations of those communities. Thus the phenomenon of the healer or wise woman appears in both societies. These societies, however, reacted in differing ways.

Many witchcraft allegations sprang from petty jealousies, local disputes and general suspicions amongst neighbours. These seem to have been articulated into a coherent form in the denunciation of the 'witch' before his or her community. Underlying social trends also played a part in such accusations. During the late sixteenth and seventeenth centuries, England was undergoing a societal metamorphosis from a largely feudal/medieval country into an early modern one. Very crudely put, it was transforming itself from medieval, rural Catholicism into a largely urban-based and increasingly widespread Protestantism. And with this gradual transformation came a change in ethos and perspective. Under the old feudal system, the emphasis was on communal help and care. Thus, the woman who lived on the edge of the village and for whom there was no employment was nevertheless certain that she would be looked after by the community around her – this was the social and religious duty of her neighbours. As a new ethos took hold, the perception shifted. The emphasis was now upon self-help and individual betterment through work. Thus, far from being looked after by her neighbours, the woman was now looked on as a drain on the community and, because she did not work, as feckless and even sinful. When an old woman came begging bread at the door of a prosperous yeoman farmer, under the old system of communal care, he would have been required to look after her. Under the new ethos, he was not – he would send her packing and she would go, probably cursing him as she did so. Later one of the farmer's animals or even one of his family might fall ill and he would externalise the guilt that he may have felt by claiming that the old woman was a witch. This change in ethos with, perhaps, concomitant externalised guilt, may have contributed to local witchcraft accusations.

It was not long before the allegations deriving from these petty spites and jealousies, changes in perspective and ethics, and localised disputes percolated all the way up to Official Statute. Although there had been many religious injunctions against witchcraft (the oldest being found in Holy Scripture in Exodus xxii: 18 – 'Thou shalt not suffer a witch to live' – with similar admonitions in the Books of Samuel, Micah and Acts), the notion did not find its way into the formal English legal mechanism by Parliamentary Act until 1541, during the reign of Henry VIII. Then it was treated, not as heresy (as on the Continent) but as a felony – *maleficium* or evil doing – for which the perpetrator was hanged and not burned (a fate reserved in England for heretics and traitors). This Act was amended during the reign of Elizabeth I in 1562 but it was in 1604, on the accession of James I (James VI of Scotland) – himself deeply superstitious and the author of one of the foremost books on witchcraft and devilry, *Daemonologie* – that a new law was enacted which contained exact specifics as to the crime of witchcraft.

It was now an offence to exercise or consult with any evil or wicked spirit or to entertain any sorcery or charm by which a person could be injured or killed, destroyed, wasted, consumed or lamed 'in his or her body or any part thereof; every such offender is a felon without benefit of clergy'. This effectively moved the emphasis of alleged witchcraft from healing to hurting and meant that many localised sicknesses and maladies could be ascribed to the anti-social activities of witches within a community. It also opened the door for accusations born of local spites, jealousies and differences of opinion.

Under this law and the methods of its administration, allegations of witchcraft rapidly increased, as did the persecutions, especially in rural areas of England. These began to become even more frequent during the period of the Commonwealth (1649-1659), particularly in the more easterly of the English counties. Many accusations, followed by executions (bearing in mind the strictures of Exodus) occurred in Lancashire, in Suffolk, in Huntingdonshire and in Essex. It was in the east of the country, around the mid-seventeenth century, that the celebrated so-called 'Witchfinder General', Matthew Hopkins, plied his trade. Hopkins claimed to have a Bill from Parliament which entitled him to examine and assess those accused of witchcraft, in order to determine whether or not they were the instruments of the Evil One. To a lesser degree, there were other such 'finders' travelling around parts of England and Scotland, seeking out and advising upon instances of witchcraft.

Although in Ireland witchcraft was viewed in a slightly different way and many 'wise women' (who might have been deemed to be witches in England) were viewed as central to local communities, this is not to say that the Irish Parliament did not take some steps to formalise witchcraft as a crime. In 1586, no doubt to bring Ireland into line with the English courts, a statute was passed outlawing the practice. This forbade the use of 'any witchcraft, enchauntment, charme or sorcery, whereby any person shall happen to be killed or destroyed' or if any person was 'wasted, consumed or lamed' or have their 'goodes and cattels' harmed through enchantment, the offender was to be treated as a felon and condemned to death. This, according to the Reverend St John Seymour in his book *Irish Witchcraft and Demonology* (1913) was basically the only statute enacted by the Irish Parliament and it is not known exactly how rigorously it was enforced. It is thought to have been used in a witchcraft trial at Kilkenny in 1578 but unfortunately no details of this case survive.

In areas of Ireland that had been widely settled by the English, English law (or an approximation thereof) prevailed. It is not unusual, therefore, to find an English-type witchcraft accusation in such an area as Youghal, County Cork, which had been extensively settled by English Puritans. Since the mid-to-late 1500s, the town had always been considered 'English' — Sir Walter Raleigh had been one of its early mayors and the first potatoes from the New World were grown in Youghal — and 'English ways' were said to prevail there. It is not altogether surprising, therefore, that English beliefs in witchcraft should also manifest themselves there in the trial of Florence Newton in 1661.

The case emerged out of a disagreement between an old woman and a young girl. Florence Newton was committed to Youghal prison by the mayor of the town on 24 March 1661, to stand trial for witchcraft at Cork Assizes on 11 September. She was accused of bewitching a servant girl, Mary Longdon, who was called to give evidence against her at her trial. Newton was a beggar woman who seldom worked and who went from house to house, scrounging what she could get from local people. It is also said that she had a bad reputation and she probably encouraged this as a means of ensuring that nobody turned her away or refused her when she called.

Mary Longdon, on the other hand, was one of the younger maidservants in the relatively prosperous household of John Pyne, a former Bailiff and later Mayor of Youghal. Popular legend says that she was forthright in her speech and, being in the service of a well-to-do gentleman, was both snobbish and forward in her manner.

Giving evidence at the Cork Assizes, Longdon asserted that on one occasion, around Christmas-time, the beggar woman Florence Newton had approached her as she was working at John Pyne's house and had asked her for a piece of beef from the powdering tub nearby. Insolently, the servant told her that she would not give away her master's beef to one such as she and told her to be on her way. It was a brave thing to do, since Mary Longdon had known Newton for about three or four years and must have been well aware of her reputation as an evil woman and a sorceress. Newton turned away grumbling, saying, 'Thou had best give it me', which was later construed as a threat of harm.

About a week later, Mary Longdon was going to fetch water with a 'pail of cloth' (a piece of cloth sometimes used by women to protect their hair when carrying pails of water) on her head when she met Newton again. Grabbing the edge of the cloth, the beggar woman threw it off her head and then violently kissed the girl, saying, 'Mary, I pray thee and I be Friends, for I bear thee no ill will and I pray thee do not thou bear me any.' Possibly shocked by this surprising action, the girl returned home but a couple of days later, she woke to find a figure whom she described as 'a Woman with a Vail over her Face' standing by her bedside. The figure was not alone for beside her stood another shape which looked to her like 'a little old Man in Silk Cloaths and … this man, whom she took to be a Spirit drew the Vail off the Woman's Face and then she knew it to be Goody Newton'. The spirit in the guise of the old man then spoke to the girl asking her to follow him and she would have 'all things after her own Heart'. Horrified at the seductions of the Tempter, the girl firmly answered 'No' and told him that she would have nothing further to say as her trust was in the Lord. The visions then vanished.

Within a month after being kissed by Florence Newton, Mary Longdon fell ill and became subject to 'fits and trances', which were of an extremely violent kind and would often come upon her very suddenly. When having these fits, she would be taken with vomiting and disgorged all manner of odd things – needles, pins, horseshoe nails, wool and straw. During these retchings she was seized by spasms that were so violent that it often required three or four strong men to hold her down.

During all these trances, she saw visions of Florence Newton who would, seemingly, approach her with the intention of sticking nails and pins into various parts of her body, particularly her arms. Indeed, it seems that there were some actual pins stuck into her forearms, some so deep and so fast that it took three or four plucks to get them out. At other times, Newton's spectre would carry her from her bed in one room to another room, sometimes she would be carried to the very top of John Pyne's house and laid amongst the rafters, sometimes on the mat in her master's chamber. At all times, she cried out against Florence Newton to stop tormenting her but the evil spirit paid her no heed. Sometimes, she claimed, she saw Newton herself, sometimes the transportation and the injuries were done invisibly. From time to time too, she claimed that she was pelted by showers of small stones, which seemed to materialise from nowhere and always when she was alone. However, there was ample evidence that she had been bruised and battered by this phenomenon.

How, she was asked, could she be sure that Florence Newton was responsible for these uncanny events? The servant girl replied that the fits and trances hadn't started until she had been kissed by Newton and that by the kiss, the old woman 'had bewitched her'. She had also sought to find out more about the beggar woman and had been advised that she was indeed a witch. She was then asked if she knew Florence Newton well and she replied that she did — she had known her for at least four years — and now wished that she did not. It is here that Newton seems to have sealed her own verdict, for as Mary Longdon finished her evidence, according to court records the old woman 'peeped at her, as it were, betwixt heads of the bystanders ... and, lifting up both her hands together, as they were manacled, cast them in a violent angry motion (as was observed by W. Aston) towards the said Mary, as if she intended to strike her if she could have reached her and said, "Now she is down". Upon which the Maid fell suddenly down to the ground like a stone, and fell into a most violent Fit, that all the people that could come and lay hands on her scarce could hold her, she biting her own arms and shreeking out in a most hideous manner to the amazement of all Beholders.' And it was noted by some who had been sitting close to her, that Newton had sat apart from the rest of the court, pinching her own arms and hands. Mary Longdon was carried out of the court to a nearby house and Florence Newton remained where she was with her manacles being loosened (or removed) to give her ease. Soon word came back to those present, that Mary had taken another violent vomiting fit and had disgorged a number of crooked pins (several of which were brought for inspection), straws, wool and a large amount of foam-like spittle. It was remarked that while Florence Newton had been chained, Mary Longdon had appeared quite well but when the manacles had been loosened, she had been taken ill. It was also remarked how Newton had scratched and pinched herself as Mary Longdon was giving her evidence and several people suggested that the beggar might have been casting some sort of spell on the girl. The jailor was instructed to bolt her manacles once more and at this the old woman cried out that she was being killed and destroyed and why were they tormenting her. But, shortly after, word came to the court that Mary Longdon had recovered and was well. Florence Newton raised her head and replied in a low voice: *'She is not well yet!'* Asked what she meant by these words, she denied that she had ever said them, although many people within the courtroom maintained that they had heard her. On being pressed, she replied that she was old and confused and had been greatly distracted by the pain of being remanacled, so she had no recollection of saying them. The entire incident, however, had not done her case any good.

An expert witness, a Mr Nicholas Stout, was then produced who declared that in his reading of several witchcraft trials it had been declared that no witch could repeat the Lord's Prayer. At this, Florence Newton interrupted the court, saying that she could recite it perfectly well. The court then gave her leave to say it. She started well enough but after *'Give us this day our daily bread'*, she missed a line and proceeded straight to *'As we forgive them'*. The court then instructed someone to teach her the omitted words *'And forgive us our trespasses'*. However, she could not, or would not, say them but simply repeated 'Ay, ay, trespasses — that's the word' over and over — a fact that the court may have found significant. She was often urged to repeat the full sentence but she did not. On being asked the reason, she repeated that she was old and had a bad memory. It was pointed out to her that she could well remember other things and that it was only a part of Holy Scripture that eluded her, to which she replied that she didn't know why she couldn't repeat it, only that she couldn't help it.

It was then decided to recall the by now recovered Mary Longdon but it was discovered that she had actually left the town and so her employer, John Pyne, was called to give evidence. He stated that in about January 1661, Mary had complained to him that she was 'much troubled' with small stones being thrown at her as well as some other items (which corroborated Mary's own statement) and that sometimes, as she read the Bible, the Holy Word was struck from her hand by an invisible force. Sometimes, the Holy Word was thrown into the middle of the room, so violent had the unseen intervention been, and Mary always experienced violent spasms and vomiting afterwards.

Another witness, Nicholas Pyne, stated that he, together with several other townsmen, had visited Florence Newton in jail on either 24 or 26 March (the date isn't clear) in order to speak with her and tell her what the citizens of Youghal were saying about her – that she was a witch and that she had cast a spell on the unfortunate girl. They asked her to be honest with them – were these things actually true? After some consideration, Newton replied that she hadn't *bewitched* the girl but had merely *overlooked* her.

There was, in the popular mind, a distinction between the two things. To bewitch somebody was to actively recite a charm or incantation against them or to deliberately prepare some form of conjuration which would do them supernatural harm. To 'overlook' them was simply to wish them ill in a forceful manner. Old women, both Irish and English, were believed to overlook the cattle of their enemies in the hope that some of them would take ill – which they usually did. Newton admitted that the kiss had been given wishing mischief on Mary Longdon and it was an act for which she was now heartily sorry. She knew that she had badly wronged Mary, she stated, and in front of them all, she now fell on her knees and begged forgiveness. But there were others in the town of Youghal, she said, who could do these things as well as she (and she named two other women – Goody Halfpenny and Goody Dod) and it might well be one of these who had afflicted the girl.

One other piece of startling information was relayed. Towards evening, Mr Pyne informed the court, the door of Newton's cell shook violently, making all the bolts rattle. From inside, Newton's voice could be heard saying: 'What makest thou here at this time o' night?' The noise then continued as if somebody were running up and down the cell and the bolts continued to rattle. On being questioned about it, Newton first of all denied that it had happened – she had seen or heard nothing, neither did she speak – but later, under some intense questioning, she confessed that she had been visited by a spirit, her 'familiar' (attendant demon), in the shape of a greyhound. The mention of the familiar once again brings in notions of English and Continental witchcraft. It was thought that Satan provided all witches with a devil to help them, and these devils were known as familiars. These sprites usually took animal form – a cat, toad, rat etc. – and stayed with the witch until she died, carrying her soul back to the Infernal Master. The case was now moving into serious territory.

The trial began to take on some of the characteristics of English witch-finding with specific examinations of the accused taking place under the supervision of supposed 'experts'. For example, in his evidence John Pyne stated that a Mr Edward Perry had secretly taken a tile from Newton's cell into a room where Mary Longdon was waiting. There he put it on the fire until it was red-hot and then dripped 'some of the Maid's water' (urine?) on it. At this point Newton, still in her cell and unaware of these proceedings, was 'grievously tormented' and cried out until the water was 'consumed', when she gained peace again. This seemed to suggest something unnatural was happening.

* * *

A new figure now appears to have become involved in the proceedings – the colourful character of Valentine Greatrakes. Greatrakes (or Greatrix as he is called in some of the records) seems to have operated in this case much in the same way as a witchfinder such as Matthew Hopkins in Essex. Nevertheless, although brought in as one of those who examined the alleged witch whilst in her cell, Greatrakes seems to have enjoyed more of a reputation as a healer than a witchfinder.

Indeed, at the time he was widely known as 'the Irish Stroker' because of his alleged powers in the laying on of hands in order to cure 'King's Evil'.

'King's Evil', or scrofula, a disease which caused open sores and sometimes disfigurements, affected a good number of the populace both in England and Ireland and, it was believed, could be cured only by the touch of the monarch. This could be done either by direct touch or by a wave of the sovereign's hand – the Cromwellians contemptuously referred to Charles I as 'the Old Stroker', claiming that he sought to cure hundreds of the diseased by waving to them from balconies but certainly not by going amongst them. Valentine Greatrakes claimed a somewhat similar power. This was a dangerous thing to do, as he could have been considered to be usurping the monarch's position and therefore committing treason. It is indicative of his colourful character that he continued to claim this.

Born on 14 February 1629, Greatrakes was a Protestant and from a relatively prosperous family of the minor gentry. Despite being described as a man 'with a friendly, sociable humour', Greatrakes also seems to have had a slightly more fanatical side – espousing some of the more extreme aspects of religion. During the period of the Commonwealth in Ireland, he joined the Parliamentarian army, becoming a lieutenant of cavalry. So highly was he considered that he was offered, and accepted, the post of High Sheriff of Waterford, incurring the enmity of many Anglicans along the way because of his views. In 1660, the Commonwealth government fell and the king, Charles II, was restored. Anglicanism was now in vogue once more and Greatrakes was unceremoniously removed from office, which left him bitter and frustrated. However, in 1663, and at the age of 34, he was to find a new outlet for his undoubted energies.

A young boy who lived close to Greatrakes and his wife was suffering from scrofula and 'at the Lord's command' the former sheriff suddenly felt compelled to lay his hands upon him in order to cure him. The child seems to have been cured and Greatrakes now felt a 'strange persuasion' (as he told his wife) to become a healer. He was certain that he had a healing touch. He began to 'heal' other afflicted people, including one, Margaret McShane, whose condition he admitted in his diary almost turned his stomach. Whether he cured by actual powers or whether by autosuggestion is open to question but he soon established a clientele for himself with sufferers beginning to seek him out.

Such a reputation brought him to the attention of the (Anglican) Dean of Lismore (in whose diocese he was living) who immediately forbade him to practise such curing any further. Greatrakes, of course, ignored the injunction – the Dean was an Anglican after all – and does not seem to have been penalised in any way, although there were rumours circulating (no doubt encouraged by the Church) that he was a fraud.

Why 'the Stroker' involved himself in the Florence Newton case is unclear but he seems to have been contacted by some of the citizenry of Youghal in an 'expert' capacity. He now professed himself to have a knowledge of witchcraft and its ways and may have claimed he knew of methods by which to interrogate suspected sorcerers.

The method suggested by Greatrakes involved a shoemaker's awl. Newton was sat on a stool in the middle of the cell and the awl was stuck into the stool about her. This may be a variant of the method of 'pricking' a witch as employed by Matthew Hopkins. It was generally agreed that when a compact was entered into with Satan, the Evil One touched the witch on some part of his or her body and thereafter, that spot was insensitive to pain. Therefore, Hopkins and other such witchhunters began to prod suspected witches with sharp implements in the hope of finding this spot and thus confirming their guilt. After repeated 'pricking', the body eventually did become insensitive and this was often taken as evidence of evil. While it is unclear if Valentine Greatrakes actually did prod Florence Newton's flesh with the awl or if he merely threatened her by plunging it into the wood of the stool, it must have been a very frightening experience for her. Indeed, in the course of these gruesome events the blade of the awl was broken to the length of about half an inch.

Her interrogators encouraged Newton to rise, but she wouldn't, saying that she was very weary. At some stage Mary Longdon was brought in to confront her alleged tormentor. Greatrakes allegedly placed the awl in Mary's hand and ran violently at Newton's hand with it but according to witnesses the awl wouldn't enter the hand and became so bent that none present could straighten it. A Mr Blackwell then produced some sort of lance and scraped Newton's hand, making a scar of about one and a quarter inches long, but no blood appeared to have been drawn. He then lanced the other hand of the accused woman and it bled readily — this was interpreted as another sign of witchcraft.

Later, Newton was again examined, this time by Edward Perry and several others. They asked her about the familiar, in the form of a greyhound, which had supposedly recently visited her in her cell. Newton initially denied that any such spirit had ever visited her but, after more intensive questioning, she finally admitted that it was indeed her familiar, that it was in the shape of an animal and that it had left through the prison window. She then said, 'If I did the Maid [Mary Longdon] any harm then I am sorry for it.' She repeated that she had not *bewitched* the girl but had simply *overlooked* her and had sealed that act with a kiss.

Evidence was also given by a minister, a Reverend James Wood, who had been summoned to attend to Mary Longdon after she had been apparently bombarded by one of the showers of small stones. Having been fetched by Mary's brother, he went to the house to find Mary herself in a fit and crying out against 'Gammer [Grandmother] Newton', stating that the old woman was close by — by her bedside — and that she was pricking and hurting her. The minister declared that he saw nobody there and when he pressed the matter, Mary got up and sent for Florence Newton. The old woman wouldn't come, said Mr Wood, pretending she herself was sick although it appeared that she was quite well. Richard Mayre, the Mayor of Youghal, then instructed Florence Newton to be brought in, whereupon Mary fell into the most violent fit once more. When Newton was removed from the room, the fits passed and Mary asked for a prayer book so that she could attend to her prayers. Florence Newton, however, was brought secretly into the room once more (where Mary could not see her and without her knowledge) and the fits recommenced. The girl remained senseless until the old woman was taken out again. On the advice of Greatrakes and Blackwell, the experiment was repeated several times with similar results.

The two women whom Newton had named – Goody Dod and Goody Halfpenny – were then brought to see Mary. Both women told her that they were not responsible for her fits and that they wished her no harm to which the girl replied: 'No, no, they are honest women, but it is Gammer Newton that hurts me, and I believe she is not far off.' (Newton had actually secretly been brought into the room at the same time and the fits started again.) Evidence against Florence Newton seemed to be mounting.

There was one other seemingly supernatural incident which weighed heavily against her. Since the alleged incident of the familiar appearing in her cell, two guards – David

Jones and Frank Beseley – had been placed to watch over her. It was alleged that one evening Newton came to the door of the cell and, reaching through an aperture in the door, kissed David Jones's right hand. The next morning, according to his wife, he returned home complaining of a pain in his right arm. He declared that he thought that he might be bewitched. The pain continued, forcing him to take to his bed, restless and ill. When he slept, he called out against Florence Newton and within fourteen days he was dead.

Confirming the story, Frank Beseley stated that David Jones had been willing to teach Newton the Lord's Prayer so that she could recite it faultlessly at her trial. The task was a difficult one, for Newton protested that she was old and her memory was failing. But Jones persevered, noting that she always stumbled on the line 'Forgive us our trespasses'. As Jones and Beseley were standing close by, Newton came to the grille of the cell door and called out: 'David. David, come hither. I can say the Lord's Prayer now.' Despite his companion's warning, David Jones went across to the door and listened to her. Once again, she stumbled on 'Forgive us our trespasses' and he had to remind her. Joyfully, she said she had a mind to kiss him for his help but the grille of the door prevented it and she would like to kiss his hand. He gave her his hand through the grille and she kissed it. It was after this that David began to feel ill and went home. Beseley visited him as he lay in bed groaning about Florence Newton and he told Beseley that 'the hag' (Newton) had him by the hand and was pulling off his arm although Beseley himself couldn't see her. Jones said: *'Do you not see the old hag? How she pulls me? Well, I lay my Death on her, she has bewitched me'*. And fourteen days after that, he was dead.

The evidence against Florence Newton was now concluded and it would appear that she was indicted on two counts — first, the bewitching of Mary Longdon and, secondly, causing the death of David Jones. The trial had been almost wholly conducted in an English manner and according to English law. It caused great interest both in Youghal and further afield and was considered to be so important that the Irish Attorney General went down to prosecute. Sadly, there is no record of the verdict and Florence Newton disappears from all records of the time. It is likely, however, that she was found guilty and was sentenced to be hanged in accordance with the punishment prescribed by English law in such matters.

* * *

Subsequently, many 'explanations' were offered for what occurred, all of them discounting witchcraft. One plausible explanation for the whole affair is that the girl, Mary Longdon, was either suffering from some form of hysteria or — as seems more likely — faked the fits in order to gain the attention of some of Youghal's most prominent citizens (she was regarded as a forward and snobbish girl in any case). David Jones, the gaoler, might have suffered from some form of hearing problem or other health condition, exacerbated by nerves while guarding an alleged witch, which may have resulted in a stroke of some sort. As for the hapless Florence Newton, she probably 'confessed' her witchcraft as a result of being bullied and browbeaten by men more far more powerful and learned than she.

Of course, it is easy, with the benefit of what we might term 'sophisticated hindsight', to dismiss these events as ludicrous or fanciful but this is also to dismiss the thinking and perspective of seventeenth-century Ireland. For the lawmakers and rulers of this society, who were the learned persons of their time, witchcraft served as an explanation for what they considered to be inexplicable events and also enabled them to cope with the changing ethos of the times. Nevertheless, the accusations surrounding Florence Newton remain fascinating even today, and offer an insight into the links between Irish and English society at the time, illustrating some of the tensions, fears and anxieties that underpinned life in a seventeenth-century Irish plantation town.

The Islandmagee Witches

THE DEVIL'S COVEN IN
EAST ANTRIM (1711)

If instances of witchcraft trials are few around the south of Ireland, they are even more difficult to locate in the north. Here, following the Plantation of Ulster, the Protestant clergy held sway in many areas and so acts of localised witchcraft were probably dealt with by local ministers and local congregations without the need to resort to formal court procedures.

Nevertheless, some cases *did* come to court and the north of Ireland lays claim to being one of the last areas of the United Kingdom to hold a witch trial. In Carrickfergus on the East Antrim coast, in the year 1711, a number of women from the nearby Islandmagee area were brought to trial on the charge of tormenting a young girl through supernatural arts. By this time, of course, belief in witches and in diabolical intervention in the world was beginning to wane and, although they were found guilty, the eventual fate of these women reflects this. The case was, however, an extremely complex one and in many ways bears a resemblance to the outbreak of witchcraft accusations that had occurred in the New England community of Salem, Massachusetts, barely two decades earlier.

Today, Islandmagee is a relatively isolated coastal area, situated near the major towns of Carrickfergus and Larne. It still has a reputation for being staunchly Protestant. In the late 1600s and early 1700s, it was even more isolated and was inhabited by strict Protestants (a good number of them Presbyterians) who considered themselves to be separate from the major communities around them, particularly the Anglican town of Carrickfergus. They retreated, in the main, into the certainty of their religion.

The area was also extremely superstitious. Although strict Protestantism frowned on 'Catholic fancies', there were tales of ghosts and fairies all through the region. A fairy fort near Larne, for example, was widely avoided by the local populace after dark for fear of passers-by being pelted by stones thrown by mischievous spirits. Locals did not frequent certain coastal roads in the area because of the ghosts and spectres that were believed to haunt them. The remoteness of the area, coupled with its dour and recalcitrant inhabitants, added to its somewhat eerie reputation.

The first stirrings of unnatural goings-on centred around the widow of the former Presbyterian minister in Islandmagee. Mrs Anne Haltridge (sometimes given as Hatteridge) was an aged woman and at the time was living with her son James in an apparently well-appointed house in the district of Islandmagee. Around September 1710, her stay there became distinctly unpleasant. Stones, turf and other objects were thrown on her bed; the curtains around the bed drew open and then closed again and the bed itself rocked and moved as if a considerable weight were bouncing up and down upon it. At the same time, pillows were whipped from beneath her head by an unseen force and the bedclothes were pulled up and down across her body, sometimes being dumped on the floor by the same invisible agent. Although a thorough search was made of the bedroom, nothing was discovered. There was some talk of spirits in a nearby ancient earthworks, but this was dismissed. However, the mysterious incidents continued for a couple of months and became so bad that the elderly woman could not bear to be left on her own.

Around 11 December, Mrs Haltridge was sitting by the fire. It was late evening and the entire house was in a kind of twilight as the light outside faded. The rest of the family were not present but, as she turned on her seat, the old woman suddenly realised that she was no longer alone in the room. A little boy appeared to have come in and was now warming himself from the blaze of the fire. He seemed to be about eleven or twelve years old, his hair tucked up under an old black bonnet set jauntily on his head, and he was wrapped in a torn blanket which trailed on the floor as he moved. Underneath he seemed to be wearing a torn vest. Mrs Haltridge couldn't really see his face as he kept the edges of the blanket pulled up about his lower jaw. Curious, and thinking that he might be some unfortunate that her son had taken in, Mrs Haltridge asked him several questions — Where was he from? What was he doing in the house? Where was he going? Was he cold or hungry? The child made no answer but, as if in response, got up from his seat and danced very nimbly around the kitchen, gesturing wildly at the terrified old woman before running out of the house into the yard and disappearing into the cowshed. Several of the workmen attempted to catch him but he evaded their capture and when they searched the shed, he couldn't be found. Nor were there any traces of him around about. He seems to have appeared once more to one of the servants who, seeing her master's dog coming in, cried out that the master was returning, where-upon the creature (whatever it was) vanished completely.

* * *

The household was not troubled with such visitations again until the following year. On 11 February 1711, old Mrs Haltridge was reading a book — usually given as Dr Wedderburn's *Sermons on the Covenant*, generally regarded as a staple of Presbyterianism — when suddenly the text was dashed from her hand by an unseen force, and fell to the floor. The old woman looked for it but couldn't find it — it seemed to have vanished into thin air. The next day, one of the maidservants, Margaret Spear, was working in the kitchen when the apparition of the small boy appeared outside and, breaking a pane of glass in the window, thrust the book through, keeping a tight hold of it. He then began to engage the astonished servant in conversation and told her that he had taken the book when everybody else was in another room and that her mistress (Mrs Haltridge) would never see it again. Finding her voice, the girl asked him if he could actually read the book, to which he replied that he could but only by adding what the Devil had taught him. Terrified, Margaret exclaimed: 'Lord bless me from thee! Thou hast got ill lear [learning].' The creature grimaced in what she took to be a malicious smile and told her that she could bless herself all she wanted but that it wouldn't save her. The creature then produced a sword and said that it would kill everybody in the house. With a scream, the maidservant fled, crying to other servants to lock the doors and bolt the windows, but the apparition merely laughed at her and advised her that it made no difference to him for he could enter the building by the smallest hole. He also claimed that he could take the form of a cat or mouse and that the Devil could make him do anything that he pleased. Stepping back out into the yard, he took a large stone and threw it through the parlour window. When the servants lifted it and tried to throw it back, it could not be hurled out through the window but bounced back into the room.

In the yard, all was commotion. The apparition had caught a turkey cock, which it threw over its shoulder, holding the bird by its tail, and with the book wrapped up in a blanket, the spectre vaulted over a wall. A few moments later, one of the maids saw the phantom attempt to kill the fowl with his sword but it managed to escape and flew away. The creature ran up and down with the book under its arm searching for it. Then, suddenly, in what seemed to be a fit of pique, it smashed a parlour window, using a club or a branch of a tree that it had found. The girl peeped out of the kitchen again to see the apparition digging with its sword in the ground. Timorously, she asked the creature what it was doing, to which it replied: 'Making a grave for a corpse which will come out of this house very soon.' He refused, however, to say who the dead person would be but, having delivered this piece of intriguing information, he disappeared over the hedge with a single leap as nimbly as a bird.

A couple of mornings later, Mrs Haltridge suddenly found that the clothes had been pulled from her bed whilst she slept and were now piled up at the foot. Servants put them back but they were pulled from her again while she dozed and thrown in a bundle in one of the corners of the room. On being replaced a third time, they were forcefully yanked off and moulded into the shape of a corpse or something that closely resembled it, lying at the foot of the bed.

As the news of what was going on in the Haltridge household spread, locals began to speculate about what was going on — it might be a trick or some sort of subterfuge. Gradually, however, opinions began to veer a little towards the supernatural. The Presbyterian minister in Islandmagee, Mr Robert Sinclair, was called upon to exorcise the house of this mischievous spirit. He arrived with two of his Elders — Mr

Man and Mr Leaths — and spent much of his time in prayer, but it seemed to have little effect. That same night, old Mrs Haltridge went up to bed, as was her custom, to the haunted room where she spent a restless time. About twelve o' clock, she was heard screaming, whereupon Mr Sinclair hurried to her side and asked her what was the matter. She answered that she had a fearful pain in the lower part of her back — almost, she said, as if somebody was sticking a red-hot knife into her.

The next morning, she was moved to another room but the pains continued, growing steadily worse. Whenever she lay down to sleep, she was jolted awake by the soreness in her back. Now there were whisperings in the locality that the old woman was somehow being bewitched and that evil powers were being used against her. The strange apparition which had tormented the house, it was suggested, was a minor demon, which had been sent to plague the God-fearing family, whilst the pains that Mrs. Haltridge had experienced were the result of malign sorcery.

By 22 February, the old lady had died. During her illness, the clothes were often pulled from the bed and unceremoniously dumped in the corner of the room, sometimes in the corpse-shape once again. On the evening that she died, however, they were removed without any fuss and were neatly folded and taken and placed in a chest upstairs. Nobody knew how they had got there. They had been removed without any noise or disturbance and without any indication to the people in the next room and were found only after a great deal of searching.

* * *

Up until this, the case looked as if it was no more than a simple case of haunting but things were to take a turn which would make it a proper case of witchcraft. A few days after old Mrs Haltridge's death, a young girl, Mary Dunbar, came to stay with the Haltridges. She seems to have come to visit Mrs Haltridge Junior and may even have been a relation of hers. She was almost eighteen at the time and was described as having 'an open and innocent countenance' and as being 'a very intelligent young lady'. Her arrival was probably timed to keep the younger Mrs Haltridge company after her mother-in-law's death, but it was to herald trouble for the entire household and community.

Strange things began to happen almost at once. On the evening of her arrival, Miss Dunbar retired to her room with a maid-companion to find that one of her travelling cases had been ransacked and the contents scattered all around the room. Several items that she had brought with her were missing and the house was searched. In the course of these investigations, an apron was discovered lying in the middle of the kitchen floor. The previous day it had been washed and put away in a cupboard but now it was inexplicably filthy and crumpled. Furthermore, it had been rolled up and tied in a number of peculiar knots (the exact number specified in subsequent recollections varied between five and nine). On loosening it, an old flannel cap which had belonged to old Mrs Haltridge was found twisted and wrapped in it. Both Mary Dunbar and young Mrs Haltridge took all of this as an evil omen and firmly declared that great evil had entered the house. Fuelled by the earlier suspicions of witchcraft and dark enchantments, tongues were already wagging as the story of the discarded apron and its sinister knots began to circulate through the community. There might be sorcery at work here, it was suggested, directed against somebody living in the house.

The following evening as she went to bed, Mary Dunbar complained of pains in her legs and no sooner had she lain down than the pains increased. She rose, screaming that someone was sticking a hot knife into her thigh, before falling to the ground in a swoon. Startled servants carried her back to bed where she recovered and lay calm. The pains seemed to have passed. About midnight, however, they returned with a vengeance and, once again, Mary Dunbar rose screaming. This time, she cried, there were people in the room with her, although when they arrived the servants could see no one, and they were hurting her with hot knives. Asked who these people were, she first of all gave no names, but as the pains obviously increased she blurted out some specific details. They were, she declared, all local women and their names were Janet Liston, Elizabeth Cellor, Janet Carson, Kate McCalmont, Janet Mean, a woman called Latimer and another whom she called Mrs. Ann. She also managed to give some descriptions of them – so detailed that they could actually be identified as women from various parts of the district.

The next day, some of the named women were sent for, but as they approached the house Mary Dunbar went into further spasms of pain. One of those who had been denounced, a woman by the name of Latimer from Carrickfergus who had been sent to Islandmagee by a dissenting minister named Adair, apparently caused an especially violent reaction in the girl whenever she even came near the dwelling. Because she had come from Carrickfergus and was not really all that well known in the district, local people assumed that she was merely a sightseer, but the girl recognised her instantly as one of her tormentors. Hauling herself up on a chair, Mary Dunbar screamed, 'O Latimer, Latimer!' and exactly described the person on the road outside before falling into another swoon. When she had recovered, a number of women (some accounts mention almost thirty) were brought in before her to see if they could deceive her regarding those that she had named. In each case, she recognised her tormentors. Every time one of them approached her, she began to scream and shriek that she was being tortured and went into spasms so great that it was feared that she would not recover from them.

Between 3 and 24 March, depositions were issued and the Mayor of Carrickfergus was called to issue a warrant for the arrest of several suspected persons. In the end, seven women were arrested. These were: Janet Mean of Braid Island; Jane

Latimer of the Irish Quarter in Carrickfergus; Margaret Mitchell of Kilroot; Catherine McCalmont of Islandmagee; Janet Liston, alias Sellar, also of Islandmagee; Elizabeth Sellar, of same (this may have been the Cellor of whom Mary Dunbar had spoken); Janet Carson, of same.

These, according to Mary Dunbar, were amongst her worst tormentors and in a statement given on 12 March – after six of these seven had been arrested – she stated that she had received no annoyance, except from a person she called 'Mrs Ann' and 'another woman who was blind in one eye'. She further stated that when she had told these phantoms that Mr Robb, the curate, was going to pray with her and for the salvation of her soul, the ghastly pair stated that he could pray all he wanted but that they would prevent her (Mary Dunbar) from hearing it, which they actually did. 'Mrs Ann' then told her that she would *never* know her name and consequently she, as chief witch, would never be discovered for no one else could see her. However, Mary Dunbar was able to give an accurate description and consequently Margaret Mitchell – reckoned to be the leader of the coven – was arrested, at which point Mary Dunbar seemed no longer to be tormented by further pains and fits. However, shortly after, she would claim that she felt a strange weight in her stomach and complained that she wished she was rid of it. The sensation passed and was a mystery to everyone.

With 'Mrs Ann' now under arrest, attention turned to her spectral accomplice, the woman who was blind in one eye.

She should have been easy to find in a tight-knit rural community like Islandmagee, but apparently she was not. An account of the time states that three disfigured women were brought in front of Mary Dunbar but she declared that she didn't know any of them and that they had never troubled her. A certain old woman, Jane Miller of Carrickfergus, who was blind in one eye, was secretly brought into the house and kept near Mary, without the former seeing her, to see if the girl would go into fits at her presence. As soon as she revealed herself, Mary fell into a frightful series of fits, lashing about and screaming so violently that strong men had to be brought in to hold her.

'For God's sake take that Devil out of the room!' screamed the girl. She was asked if this was one of her tormentors and she said that it was. Surprisingly, Jane Miller doesn't seem to have been arrested.

Evidence was, however, taken against the seven women now in custody. One of the statements given concerned Janet Liston who, when being summoned to attend Mary Dunbar (being at the house of a certain William Sellar of Islandmagee), refused to go. If God had taken health from her, she declared, then God would give it back to her — if the Devil had taken it then the Devil would give it to her. 'O misbelieving ones,' she added, 'eating and drinking damnation to themselves, crucifying Christ afresh, and taking all out of the hands of the Devil.' It was said that Liston was a particularly religious woman but even so Mary Dunbar maintained that she was certain in her accusations and Janet Liston was arrested. The finger of suspicion was also pointed at other women in the area but none, apart from the seven explicitly identified by Mary Dunbar, were taken into custody.

With the alleged witches arrested, a trial date was set – 31 March 1711. The two judges appointed to hear the case were Justices Upton and McCartney. Much of what we know about the court proceedings comes from the pen of the Reverend Dr Tisdall, the Anglican Vicar of Belfast who attended throughout. A high churchman, Dr Tisdall's rather disparaging views on Presbyterianism were well known but, even so, the account seems honest and balanced.

Preliminary evidence was given to the court concerning Mary Dunbar's fits which were said to be so violent that it took a number of strong men to hold her down. During these fits, she had threatened to swallow her tongue and had torn at her clothing and at her throat. She had told several witnesses that during these severe bouts it had been one of the accused, Janet Mean, who had been tormenting her. Mean was troubled with arthritis and had hands which were crooked like a bird's claws – 'so the better to torment her with'. Mean herself was called to the bar of the court and was asked to show her hands and the crowd at court gasped when they saw how accurate Mary Dunbar's description had been. The hands were hooked, with long uncut nails, so that they did indeed resemble the talons of a predatory bird. Her joints were twisted and the hands looked partly withered.

There was also further strange evidence of what seemed to be occult practices. One of the witnesses said that he had seen worsted yarn tied around Mary Dunbar's wrists and ankles, even though there was no visible agent doing this. It was put on awkwardly, as if the invisible agent had crippled hands (the implication concerning Mean was obvious). Also, the yarn had been tied in a peculiar way, using a strange knot arrangement. Apparently, this was a sure sign of witchcraft and it boded ill for her.

Either Mary Dunbar's mother or young Mrs Haltridge had been advised by a Roman Catholic priest that a charm could be used in order to defend the girl from such sorcery. Some words from the first chapter of St John's Gospel were to be written on a thin piece of paper which was to be bound up, using a complicated series of knots, thought to have been seven double and one single, which were created in a particular order, around the victim's neck. This would turn away any evil or malicious spell. Mary herself declined but at some stage during the proceedings, one of those present in the room used it. The counter-charm brought on the most violent of fits and Mary suffered the most terrible pains in the lower part of her back. Indeed, the pain was so great that she had to be held down by several burly men. The idea was circulated that the charm hadn't worked because it came from the lips of a Roman Catholic priest. During this fit, Mary slid off the bed in an unaccountable manner and this was taken as further evidence that malign supernatural forces were at work. On her recovery, she told them that she had been pulled 'this way and that' by persons whom they could not see but who were acting for the alleged witches who were still in prison. These spirits had actually tried to carry her from the room and out through the window but on hearing the name of God being used, they had dropped her to the floor. Good faith and holy prayers within the room, she revealed, had kept the spirits of the witches themselves from crossing the threshold and tormenting her so they had tried to bring her out. They also tried to make her walk into the fire which was burning in the chamber, and so injure herself. Some of those who gave evidence stated that at this time there was such a strong smell of brimstone in the room that they could hardly bear it.

During the course of the trial, a number of items were presented to the court which, it was claimed, Mary Dunbar had vomited up during her fits. These included a vast quantity of feathers, some pins, bits of cotton and yarn and two exceptionally large waistcoat buttons, almost as big as the palm of a man's hand. Some witnesses gave evidence that they had seen these things come out of her mouth but, in the case of the buttons, it was difficult to see how they could have fitted into her throat. Nevertheless, they were accepted as evidence.

* * *

The time came when Mary herself was to be called in order to give evidence. The night before she was to do so, she claimed, phantasms of at least some of the imprisoned women approached her bedside and warned her that she would not be able to give evidence against them. Consequently, when she woke in the morning, she appeared to have been struck dumb. She therefore had to sit in the courtroom throughout the trial, saying nothing, but also suffering no fit when the accused were near her. Several times it looked as if she *might* have a fit and a number of encouragements were made for her to try and give her evidence, but each time she refused by shaking her head. A few times, she attempted to stand but on each occasion she sank back into the arms of an onlooker and had to be revived.

The trial proceeded with various witnesses who had attended the girl at various times giving evidence to the court. These included several locally notable clergymen — Mr Skeffington, the curate of Larne; Mr Ogilvie, the Presbyterian minister of Larne; Mr Adair, the Presbyterian minister of Carrickfergus; Mr Cobham, the Presbyterian minister of Braid (Broad) Island and Mr Edmonstone of Red Hall, all of whom hinted at supernatural happenings.

The women themselves were now brought forward. They had no lawyer to represent them and were forced to conduct their own defence. They all categorically denied all allegations of witchcraft stating that they had been wrongly accused. Several of them were 'not good to look upon' (this may mean that they were ill-looking or that some of them were probably disfigured in some way) and were therefore all the more suspect of evil-doing. However, testimony was given that they were 'good and industrious people', that they 'prayed every day with their families both in private and public' and that every one of them was a Presbyterian. This concluded all the evidence and it was noticeable that at no time did Mary Dunbar herself take the stand. When attempts were made to get her to give evidence, she always signalled that her tongue had been magically twisted and that she could not speak.

The senior of the two judges, Judge Upton, summed up and instructed the jury that on the balance of the evidence presented, the jury could not reasonably return a guilty verdict. The main allegation had been based entirely on one person's testimony and all supporting evidence had been purely circumstantial. He said that he did not doubt that some diabolical force had been at work in Islandmagee but if the seven accused were indeed witches, they could not have prayed so earnestly nor 'publicly attended upon the Divine Service'. The judgement was a fair and humane one and in line with the evidence presented but, unfortunately, Judge McCartney did not agree with him. In his addendum, he suggested that the seven might well be guilty as witches. This was the verdict that the jury brought in.

In sentencing, Judge Upton seems to have shown a little of the same measure of humanity as in his summing-up. Under Statute, he could have sentenced the women to hang. Instead, they were given one year's imprisonment in Carrickfergus jail, perhaps an indication as to the changing mood of the times. But they were also condemned to stand in the public pillory in

Carrickfergus market square, four times during that period. On such occasions they were pelted by the common mob with eggs, tomatoes, stones, potatoes and cabbage stalks. Indeed, so vicious was the attack on them during one such occasion that one of the defendants actually lost an eye. What became of the seven women upon their release is unknown — perhaps they simply returned to their rural lives in Islandmagee, although this is doubtful.

The Islandmagee witchcraft case is counted as being the last such formal trial for actual sorcery in Ireland. Subsequent trials — such as an alleged trial against Biddy Early in Ennis, County Clare, in the 1860s — concerned the *pretence* of witchcraft for personal gain.

In fact, all over the British Isles, both popular and legal attitudes were changing with regard to accusations of sorcery. Where once such allegations would have been wholeheartedly embraced, both the ordinary populace and judges were becoming much more circumspect. The notorious Salem witch trials in America in 1692 had shown how communal hysteria could quickly spiral out of control with traumatic consequences for the entire community. This lesson was not lost on the populace back in England and Ireland. So, whilst the Islandmagee case showed many similarities to that of Salem — young women claiming supernatural attack, the alleged vomiting of yarn and cotton, a hysterical reaction when the accused were brought into court — the outcome was quite different. Furthermore, the notion of a compact with the Devil, which was a feature of Continental and Scottish Presbyterian witchcraft allegations, was dismissed. Whilst the supposed power of the Devil in a rural community was not denied, it was not seen as a central plank of the accusation. Therefore, by implication, the notion of a coven of witches operating in the area was also dismissed.

* * *

The Islandmagee case must be seen as one of the trials which marked the terminal decline of a belief in witchcraft throughout Great Britain. The following year, 1712, an old woman, Jane Wenham, known as the Witch of Walkenham (Wakenerne), was brought for trial in Hertfordshire on a charge of bewitching the household of a local clergyman. The Magistrate, Chief Justice Powell, 'a bluff but reasonable man', dismissed the notion of witchcraft and mocked the charges brought against her. Even so, the jury found her guilty and he was obliged to condemn her to death. However, she received a royal pardon shortly afterwards and was released.

The last witch execution in the British Isles was that of Janet Horne, the Witch of Durnoch in Sutherland, Scotland, in 1722. Old, strange in her ways, reclusive and probably feeble-minded, she was charged with turning her only daughter into a pony and riding her all through the night, thus accounting for the girl's deformed hand. She was found guilty and burned at Loth in Sutherland. This is generally regarded as the last formal witch burning anywhere in the

British Isles (excluding the tragic case of Bridget Cleary in Tipperary, over one hundred and fifty years later, which is dealt with in the next chapter).

As the new scientific and philosophical theories which were to characterise what we now call the Enlightenment began to take hold across much of Europe, the notions of witchcraft and sorcery which had formerly held sway began to be regarded as 'credulous and superstitious'. As the new age dawned, attacks against godly ideals were seen to take on different forms — through scientific discoveries and philosophical processes — and not simply by doing deals with the Devil in return for besting one's neighbours. The Islandmagee incident came at a time when old attitudes were dying and new ones were coming to the fore. In many ways, the trial in Carrickfergus must be seen as part of a 'closing down' process — the last kick of old ways and old beliefs against an oncoming tide of modernisation. Perhaps, in some ways, that is the final and lasting impression of Islandmagee.

...now some time ago... raised close links with...

Bridget Cleary

'THE CLONMEL WITCH BURNING' (1895)

Although nowadays we tend to think of witchcraft as being something that belongs to some distant and more barbarous time – usually the medieval or dark ages – the last 'witch burning' in the British Isles was much more recent than that. And it happened in Ireland. The burning of Bridget Cleary in Ballyvadlea, near Clonmel in County Tipperary, occurred as recently as 1895 and was widely reported in the newspapers of the day.

The case, which provoked widespread interest at the time (the noted writer, E.F. Benson, author of the celebrated *Mapp and Lucinda* books, wrote an article on the incident in the highly influential journal *The Nineteenth Century*) is a curious amalgam of folk-belief, local fears and fairy lore. A belief in witchcraft, fairy abductions and malign powers was still deeply rooted in the local mind, and this was to have terrifying and fatal results.

The notion of fairies being involved with alleged witches was not unique to southern Tipperary. Indeed, in many parts of rural Ireland, the two were inextricably linked. Wise women and 'fairy doctors' (rural healers), it was believed, had received their knowledge and skills from the Little People (fairies) and maintained close links with them. It was also believed that fairies intervened more frequently in human affairs than was commonly supposed. From time to time, it was said, they might even spirit individuals away to live with them for a time and 'teach them things'. In some cases a representation of the person – a 'stock' – might be left in their place in order to trick the community into believing that the person concerned was actually still amongst them. Small children and newborn babies were particularly at risk of such abductions until they were baptised, but even adults who had perhaps committed some sin might be 'taken away' as well.

The physical appearance of those who had been 'taken' often changed. This change was very apparent in babies and the very young – children who had been healthy-looking the evening before were often found thin, wrinkled and wasted in the morning. In many cases, the notion of being changed for a 'stock' often helped to explain the sudden onset and effects of infant tuberculosis. At one time, during an epidemic of the disease in the Burren region of County Clare, the physical appearance of the victims was put down to the fact that they'd been stolen by fairies or evil entities. Adults too could be stolen and a formerly healthy individual could be replaced with a withered, moaning thing. This was a central aspect of the Ballyvadlea witchcraft burning, where the victim was believed to have become possessed by a malevolent fairy or demonic presence.

The incident itself needs to be seen in the context of a spate of

Irish 'changeling' incidents that had spanned the nineteenth century. In County Kerry, *The Morning Post* reported the following account from Tralee Assizes in July 1826.

'Ann Roche, an old woman of very advanced age, was indicted for the murder of Michael Leahy, a young child, by drowning in the [River] Flesk. This case turned out to be a homicide committed under the delusion of the grossest superstition. The child though four years old could neither stand, walk (n)or speak – it was thought to be fairy struck – and the grandmother ordered the prisoner and one of the witnesses, Mary Clifford, to bathe the child every morning in that pool of the River Flesk where boundaries of three farms met; and on the last morning, the prisoner kept the child under the water longer than usual, when her companion (the witness Mary Clifford) said to the prisoner "How can you ever hope to see God after this?", to which the prisoner replied that "the sin was on the grandmother and not on her". Upon cross-examination, the witness said that it was not done with intent to kill the child but to cure it – to put the fairy out of it.

The policeman who apprehended her stated that, on charging her with drowning the child, she said that it was no matter if it had died four years ago.

Baron Pennefeather said that although it was a case of suspicion, and required to be thoroughly examined into, yet the jury would not be safe in convicting the prisoner of murder, however strong their suspicion might be. Verdict – Not guilty.'

The court's 'not guilty' verdict (at the direction of the judge) is suggestive of the depth of belief in changelings and 'fairy-struck' people within the community, yet the countryside around Glen-flesk was not the only region in which such superstitions manifested themselves.

On 30 January 1888, a woman named Johanna Doyle appeared at Assizes near Killarney, again on a charge of child murder. At the time she was roughly forty-five years of age, could neither read nor write and was barely able to speak any English whatsoever. She was charged with butchering her own mentally retarded son, Patsy, with a hatchet. In this terrible act, she had been aided by her husband and three of her other children. During her trial she insisted, in Irish, that thirteen-year-old Patsy had been both 'a fairy and a devil', having been 'changed' by the fairies for some malign purpose. The family had been dogged by strange events in recent years and this had been put down to Patsy's sorcerous influence. Another son, twelve-year-old Denis, described as 'an imbecile', was also considered to be under threat for a similar reason. Johanna Doyle was placed in the Killarney asylum, where she had to be restrained from hurting herself and tearing her clothes. Her eighteen-year-old daughter Mary went on record as saying that she was not surprised to hear that her mother had killed Patsy: 'I heard people say that he was a fairy and I believed them.'.

Such incidents were not confined to County Kerry. A series of changeling-related incidents appears to have occurred in County Tipperary around the mid-to-late 1800s. There are, for example, several alleged instances around Roscrea in the north of the county which seemingly took place around the 1860s but no definite information on them has been recorded.

But it was in the south of the county that the most serious instances concerning changelings seem to have occurred. *The Daily Telegraph* dated 19 May 1884 notes an arrest of two women in Clonmel, on the suspicion of having harmed a three-year-old child named Philip Dillon. When taken before a local magistrate, Anastasia Bourke and Ellen Cushion stated that they believed the child, who didn't have the use of his limbs, to be one of the fairy kind left in exchange for the original infant. Whilst the mother was absent, they entered the house and, seizing the unfortunate child, placed him naked on an iron shovel, holding him over a hot fire (a common way in rural areas to drive out malign creatures and spirits). In this way they hoped to 'break the charm' and destroy the changeling's powers. The boy was badly burnt and at the time of the newspaper report was in a very serious condition. The prisoners were remanded in custody to stand trial (no further account exists) and during the hearing they were hooted and sneered at by locals.

The most notorious case, however, also comes from the Clonmel area and concerns Bridget Cleary, who has been ignominiously dubbed 'Ireland's last witch'. The horrific events that surround her death have been recorded as the 'last witch burning in the British Isles' and have often been cited by English writers as evidence of profound ancient superstition still existing in the Irish countryside during the late nineteenth century.

Bridget Cleary was born and died in the then relatively remote Ballyvadlea area near Clonmel, south Tipperary. She was only twenty-six years old at the time of her death in 1896 and, according to *The Cork Examiner*, she had been a pretty woman of medium height and of a strong and independent cast of mind. Her parents, Patrick and Bridget Boland, belonged to the poor Catholic rural labouring classes. They were devoutly religious and extremely superstitious. This was not surprising, considering the area in which they lived.

Ballyvadlea was steeped in folklore and tradition. All through the area, the remnants of ancient earthen forts and tumuli hinted at the lore and secrets of former peoples while, from the road which ran through the district, the traveller could see the distant slopes of Slievenamon, the fairy-haunted mountain, once said to be the stronghold of the legendary Fenian knights, where all manner of supernatural creatures were said to dwell. Between its lower slopes and Fethard town, many 'slieveens' lived. They were the 'fairy doctors' or 'cunning men' (in its modern usage the term 'slieveen' is now taken to mean 'rascal' or 'trickster' and is a term of abuse) who were intimately familiar with the ways of the Little People and who displayed skills that verged on the supernatural. These were men like Denis Ganey, who resided in a reputedly well-appointed thatched cabin at Kyleatlea on the mountainside, or John (Jack) Dunne, a limping, toothless man who tramped the streets of both Clonmel and

Fethard, telling tales of both fairies and ghosts.

There were fairy-haunted sites everywhere in the locality. At certain times of the year, Slievenamon itself was reputedly frequented by witches and enchanters from all over Ireland. Close to where the Bolands lived rose the brooding bulk of Kylenagranagh Hill, which was topped with a fairy fort or rath — reputedly a 'sheehoguey' place (a site of supernatural dread) where the *Sidhe* or the fairy host held court and plotted mischief against the humans who lived around them. Local people simply avoided the place — beliefs connecting such sites with supernatural dangers ran very deep amongst them.

* * *

Although a strong-willed and opinionated young woman, Bridget Boland does not appear to have felt the need to move away from her narrow rural environment. Always good at sewing and stitching, she became a self-employed dress-maker, working from home. Indeed, as her father was to state later, she became one of the first women in Ballyvadlea to own a new Singer sewing machine, which she kept in her bed-room. Her new business venture seems to have been popular throughout the local community and soon Bridget Boland was relatively prosperous, which added to her desirability amongst the young men in the surrounding townlands of Ballyvadlea, Cloneen and Mullinahone. She could have had her pick of any of them. A stylish young woman by all accounts, it appears that she was noticed by one of the local landowners who, on his way to hunt with the Tipperary Hounds, had been so struck by her attractiveness as she passed him on the road that he had asked who she was and later claimed that the memory of her had stayed with him into old age. Her prettiness had also turned the heads of many of the young labourers in the area. However, the man she chose as her husband came as a surprise to the entire community. He was Michael Cleary, a dark, brooding character, almost ten years older than herself.

It is thought that Bridget and Michael met in Clonmel town. She was doing some apprentice work in a milliner's there whilst he was working as a cooper (barrel-maker). He was a dark and sullen man who reputedly had never bothered much with women and was highly superstitious. He was, for example, wary of his wife's mother, Bridget Keating, who had been considered to be a 'fairy woman' who had been 'taken' several times and who had as a result been somewhat distrusted. He was an unlikely partner for the independent Bridget Boland. Even so, they were married in August 1887 when Bridget was eighteen and Michael was twenty-seven. It was an unusually young age for Bridget, as most Irish women of the time delayed getting wed until they were around twenty-six. In fact, there was a surplus of unmarried women all across Ireland. The marriage was even more strange, because for some time after the wedding Michael continued to live and work in Clonmel while Bridget returned home every evening to her parents' house near Ballyvadlea Bridge.

The reason for this may have been that Bridget was needed at home to look after her mother who was ill (the older woman died around 1893) but there were other rumours too. Some people in the area suggested that Bridget might be seeing some-one else and the general consensus was that it was one of her neighbours, William Simpson. If such an affair existed (and there is absolutely no evidence that it did), there were good rea-sons for keeping it quiet. Simpson was married and lived with his wife Mary (known as Minnie) and two children in a farm-house a few hundred yards from the Clearys. He is described as an 'emergencyman' (a form of land steward) and as such was 'not the sort of man you could easily make friends with'. He and his family occupied a farm from which the landlord, his employer, had evicted the previous tenants some years before. But there was something else — the Simpsons were Protestants and, in a conservatively Catholic area, the idea of a young Catholic girl consorting with a married Protestant was scandalous if not unthinkable. There was probably no truth at all in the rumours but it fitted in well with what some local people considered to be Bridget's 'high and mighty' attitude. If the stories about his wife ever reached Michael Cleary in Clonmel, he appeared to take no heed of them.

A little while after Bridget's marriage, the Cashel Poor Law Guardians erected a new cottage in the district under the 1883 Labourer's (Ireland) Act. This was designed to be suit-able for a labouring family and was built about half a mile up the hill from Ballyvadlea Bridge in the townland of

Tullowcossaun. From the door and front window it had a direct view across the countryside to distant Slievenamon. It was a fine, modern structure with a high sloping, slated roof and a chimney at each gable and, as such, was considered much grander than the cabins roundabout. There was one drawback, however. It had been built on the site of an old fairy rath and the immediate area was widely regarded as a supernatural site. Such a reputation deterred many locals from applying for its tenancy.

Nevertheless, in the late 1880s, Bridget and Michael Cleary, supported by Bridget's parents, applied to the Guardians for tenancy of the new cottage. They were unsuccessful and the place was given to another labourer. Shortly after he moved in, the place fell vacant again, allegedly due to 'certain problems'. It is unclear what these 'problems' might have been but it was said that the fairies had taken exception to the occupancy and has disturbed the man with unearthly cries and shrieks. He quickly moved out. Once again, the Clearys applied for tenancy of the cottage and this time they were successful. It is unknown when they took up occupancy but it is suspected that their move created some local resentment — after all, compared to many of their neighbours the couple were regarded as reasonably well-off, and furthermore Bridget was thought to have 'airs' about her. The new cottage reflected their supposedly 'grand' status in relation to their neighbours. Despite Bridget's airs, the family soon fell into arrears of rent — not an uncommon thing in the district, but puzzling given the Clearys' relatively prosperous status. In fact, they were so badly in arrears that the Poor Law Guardians forbade any repair work to be carried out on the cottage until the debt was cleared.

At Tullowcossaun, they were surrounded by relatives. Mary Kennedy, Patrick Boland's widowed sister and Bridget's aunt, lived a short distance away at Ballyvadlea Bridge. Her sons Patrick, James and William, all labouring men, lived with her, as did her eleven-year-old granddaughter, Katie Burke, who was her daughter Johanna's eldest child. Johanna herself lived nearby with her husband Michael Burke, also a labourer, and several other children. Bridget had been Johanna's bridesmaid and the two women were reasonably close, despite Johanna being some years older than her cousin (at the time of Bridget's death she was about thirty-four years old). Johanna Burke was known as 'Han' or 'Hannie' to her family and friends.

From the time she came to live at Tullowcossaun, Bridget continued to show a strong and independent spirit. Michael was still working in Clonmel and it was up to her to run the house and provide for her widowed father after her mother's death. She still did some dressmaking, although not as much as before, but she now had another source of income – she kept hens. Hens and their eggs were an important source of income to any household and it enabled Bridget to be more or less financially independent from her husband and set a tidy sum of money by for herself. She sold 'on tick', collecting the money for her produce around the start of each month. There were some problems with this arrangement, however, as not everybody was willing or able to pay her when she called and some of her neighbours had soon run up large bills.

The winter of 1894/95 was bitterly cold and severe, all through South Tipperary. Snow and ice, coupled with hard frosts, delayed farm work long after Christmas, and many labourers found themselves without wages and facing the prospect of serious debt and destitution. It was not until late March that the weather picked up again and working conditions improved. For the Clearys, the situation was not so desperate — not being a labourer, Michael was not dependent on seasonal work like his neighbours, but for Bridget the impact was slightly more serious. If money was scarce throughout the countryside, payment from eggs already sold would be hard to come by.

*　*　*

On Monday, 4 March 1895, Bridget Cleary walked from her home in Tullowcossaun, across Ballyvadlea Bridge, towards a squalid cabin near Kylenagranagh Hill. It was here that the 'fairy man' Jack Dunne (a first cousin of her father's) lived with his wife Kate, and Bridget was calling on them to collect outstanding money for eggs. Winter still had a firm grip on the land and although the day was dry it was very cold. The weather had settled into an awkward pattern — bitter days filled with snow and sleet, followed by three or four milder ones with wind and rain. The country people said that it wasn't a healthy time. It had been snowing the night before and, as she walked, Bridget could see that the peak of distant Slievenamon was white in the morning sun. Dunne's dwelling was a rough, narrow roadside hut and as she drew nearer, it appeared to be empty. Jack and Kate Dunne had no children and spent much of their time in the pubs of Clonmel or Fethard, leaving their cabin empty for long periods. Bridget knocked at the door but there was no reply. She waited for a while, feeling the cold penetrating her clothes, then walked home again and entered her own house shivering. She tried to warm herself in front of the open fire but, according to her cousin Johanna Burke, it was no use. She had caught what the country people called a 'founder', a severe and penetrating chill.

The shivering fit hadn't passed, even by the next day, and Bridget now complained of a severe headache. Great attention was paid to the place where she had received the 'founder' and her reasons for being there. Living near the sinister Kylenagranagh Hill, Jack Dunne was said to be 'well in' with the fairies, and was widely regarded as a *shanachie*, a teller of stories (mainly ghost stories) and a custodian of ancient lore. He claimed to have seen the fairies on numerous occasions playing hurling near his back door in the last light of the evening. In the pubs, he frequently complained of an awful pain in his back, which he said had occurred one night when the fairies had lifted him bodily out of his bed and had thrown him out into the yard. A couple of times he had been chased into his house by a man in black and a woman in white who were undoubtedly of the fairy kind. He claimed to know the fairies intimately and had even been up Kylena-granagh Hill with them. Such talk often secured drinks for him and his wife and he was treated with a great deal of awe and respect. To demand money from a man who was so friendly with the fairies might be to invite disaster. Maybe *that* was what Bridget Cleary's 'founder' was all about.

Bridget went to bed to see if she could recover from the chill that she'd caught at Jack Dunne's door. There was no sign of improvement and if anything her condition grew slowly worse. It is possible that she may have caught pneumonia but she remained untreated. Doctors in the country areas around Clonmel were few and far between and were very expensive. Far better to fetch the 'fairy doctor' and see if he could cure the chill. And so it was that Jack Dunne himself made his way to Tullowcossaun. Ostensibly, he came as a relative and neighbour to see how she was but, as a man connected to the fairies, he was probably also called upon to make an unofficial 'diagnosis' to see what might be wrong with her and how best she might be cured. Although able to sit at the fire, take some food and walk around a little bit, Bridget was still feverish and was certainly not her former confident, attractive, well turned-out self. Dunne sat with her for a little while but the room was probably dark and his eyesight was not what it had been. Squinting in the smoky light, the old man looked at the young woman. His words were to have a dramatic effect on subsequent events.

'That is not Bridget Boland,' he whispered, using her maiden name. In other circumstances such a remark might have been taken differently. Jack Dunne could easily have meant 'she's not looking like herself today' or 'she's badly failed', but coming from the lips of a 'fairy man', these words had a particular resonance. Jack Dunne was actually articulating what a number of people were thinking anyway — that the real Bridget had been somehow spirited away and had been replaced by a 'stock' or 'pattern' of herself. This was no longer a human woman but a 'sheehoguey' thing that had come down from Kylenagranagh Hill to take her place. Bridget, of course, had a number of enemies amongst her neighbours — those who were envious of her, suitors that she'd snubbed and those who thought that she was too 'high and mighty' — and some of them had been remarking on how a proud and independent woman had suddenly turned into a weak and insipid invalid who could not even go out of the house. The reason for such sudden and rapid deterioration had to be a supernatural one. There was one other indication that this might be the case — although they had been married for over seven years, Michael and Bridget Cleary were still childless, a sure hint of fairy involvement.

Following Dunne's assertions, he was asked to look at the invalid more closely and he immediately suggested that she was indeed a fairy. One leg, he stated, was longer than the other (a condition which was not dissimilar to Dunne's own) which was a sure sign that she was 'fairy-struck'. Whilst he was measuring Bridget, Michael Cleary arrived at the house to find him there. He paid close attention to everything Jack Dunne had to say, taking the old man's opinions (strange though they were) to heart.

'This is not my wife at all. This is not Bridget,' Michael muttered to himself. 'It's a fairy-creature from Kylenagranagh Hill.' But although he was suspicious, he did nothing about it.

* * *

Bridget's condition worsened over the next few days. By Saturday 9 March, she was barely able to stir herself from her bed. Her cousin Johanna Burke believed that she'd caught a fresh chill or that the 'founder' had got a real hold on her. Despite the 'consultation' with Jack Dunne it was considered that a trained medical doctor should be sent for. Patrick Boland walked the four miles to Fethard to ask Dr. William Crean to call at the house and look at his daughter. On his journey to the doctor's surgery, he stopped at the house of one of the Poor Law Guardians to get the 'red ticket', which entitled Bridget to a medical examination under the Poor Law scheme. He then walked to the Dispensary in Fethard and asked Crean to visit the house.

The weekend passed and the doctor still had not come. The weather was changing – gales were blowing and the days were dull and wet; the road into Ballyvadlea was muddy and covered with blown-down branches and leaves. Perhaps Crean didn't fancy travelling into that remote area on what he might have considered to be a 'charity case'; perhaps he was busy elsewhere. There were also stories that the good doctor was a bit too fond of the bottle for his own good and that he attended to his medical duties in a haphazard fashion. From late Sunday and all through Monday, it rained very heavily, nearly flooding the roads, but as the evening wore on, it began to ease. There was still no sign of Dr Crean but, all the while, Bridget's condition appeared to grow steadily worse. Johanna Burke was convinced that she now had a fever and that a doctor must be brought as a matter of urgency. On Monday afternoon, Michael Cleary himself walked all the way to Fethard to remind the doctor, but still Crean didn't come. Nor did he come on Tuesday.

On Wednesday, 13 March, Michael Cleary again walked the four miles to Fethard to see if the doctor would come, and he also sent a message to Drangan chapel to ask Father Cornelius Ryan if he would come to attend to his wife who was dying. This did the trick, and on Wednesday afternoon Dr Crean finally called at the Cleary home. His examination may have been a cursory one and the diagnosis swift and perfunctory. Bridget was suffering from 'nervous excitement', coupled with a slight bronchitis. He prescribed a medicine and went back to Fethard. Later, at Michael Cleary's trial, he would reveal that he didn't know if the family had actually obtained the medicine, nor could he give any cause for the 'excitement'. But he would reveal that Bridget had been attending his surgery in Fethard for 'about six to eight months', although he didn't say why. The popular belief was that she had a tubercular condition and that she had been attending the TB clinic in Clonmel.

Bridget's illness was now beginning to have an impact on the immediate family — Michael Cleary was sinking deeper and deeper into depression and Patrick Boland was becoming increasingly worried about his daughter's condition. He asked his sister, Mary Kennedy, to call on her and she said that she would bring Johanna Burke who lived nearby at Rathkenny. When Han Burke arrived, both she and Bridget got into an earnest conversation and Johanna was of the opinion that there was some sort of marital difficulty between Bridget and her husband, but this remained unspecified. 'He's making a fairy of me,' complained the invalid. In local parlance, this meant that Michael Cleary was distancing himself from her for some reason. Johanna Burke also knew that Michael Cleary had had frequent disagreements with his mother-in-law and that he thought that the 'fairy woman' had passed on some of her rumoured arcane powers and skills to her daughter, making the brooding and superstitious man nervous of his wife.

Even with these visitors and the almost forced merriment going on in the house, Bridget's condition didn't improve. If she was taking Doctor Crean's medicine, it had no apparent effect on her. As he looked from his doorway to distant Slievenamon, Michael Cleary wondered what he should do about his wife. He had tried to bring Doctor Crean to the house no less than three times and when he finally did come, his diagnosis had been unsatisfactory. There was another option of course – Jack Dunne had suggested that the family consult with Denis Ganey, a 'fairy man' over in Kylatlea on the lower slopes of the mountain. And so, on Thursday, 14 March, Michael Cleary set out for Slievenamon.

According to contemporary accounts, Denis Ganey was a middle-aged man, rather tall and with a heavy beard. Like Jack Dunne and several other 'fairy men', he walked with a limp, having one leg shorter than the other. According to Michael Cleary, Ganey listened very attentively, asking several questions about Bridget's condition and then handed over something 'with nine herbs in it' which, he claimed, would drive the fairy out of Michael's wife.

The meeting with Ganey had a powerful effect on Cleary and he returned home in a highly agitated state. It is reasonable to suppose that the 'cure' that he'd obtained from 'Ganey over the mountain' probably contained lusmore (foxglove) which was supposed to 'burn the entrails out of any fairy or unearthly creature'. It had to be mixed with the 'beestings', the first milk drawn from a cow directly after calving into a bucket in which a silver coin had been placed. If the charm *did* contain a substantial amount of foxglove, then it was poisonous, and would only have worsened Bridget's condition. But Michael Cleary, who apparently believed in charms and 'fairy potions', was determined that she should have it. After the meeting with Denis Ganey, he was now more convinced than ever that Bridget was a changeling and that, if not dealt with, she would work a malign influence on him and his family. Perhaps it was Ganey who had put the notion in his head, but he was now convinced that the *real* Bridget Cleary had been abducted by the fairy kind and was now being held prisoner somewhere beneath Kylenagranagh Hill, having been replaced by some awful supernatural Thing that had to be driven out.

That same evening, a crowd of neighbours, including the Burkes and the Simpsons, called at the Cleary house to see how Bridget was. As they approached the building, they heard a man's voice from inside shout angrily: 'Take that, you rap!' Pausing outside the place, a couple of them tried to look in through the window but the shutters were drawn and they could see nothing. They knocked on the door, but from inside Michael Cleary's voice told them that they couldn't come in yet. For some minutes, the neighbours waited outside the door whilst voices inside the house screamed and shouted. They heard snatches of a heated conversation — 'Take it, you old bitch!' or 'Take it, you witch!' Then, to everyone's surprise, the door suddenly flew open and from somewhere inside a man's voice cried: 'Away she go! Away she go!' Michael Cleary came to the doorway, apparently bathed in sweat, and invited his neighbours in. They looked at him strangely and he explained that he had kept the door closed because the house had been full of fairies.

One of the first through the door was Johanna Burke and,

she was to say later, the scene that greeted them was one of brutal horror. Patrick Boland was sitting in the kitchen by the light of a large oil lamp, but everyone else was in the bedroom. Bridget Cleary was lying on the bed with Jack Dunne (who was not a sturdy man), forcibly holding her head down by the ears. Her cousin Patrick Kennedy was on the far side of the bed, gripping her right arm, whilst his brother James held her left. The younger brother, William, lay across her legs to prevent her from moving them and from trying to get up. They were forcing her to take something on a spoon from a small black saucepan which Jack Dunne called 'a pint'. Later, a report in the *Irish Times*, covering Michael Cleary's trial, stated:

'Cleary was giving her medicine – some herbs on a spoon. Bridget Cleary was trying not to take it. She said that it was too bitter. When Cleary put the milk into the mouth, he put his hand on her mouth to prevent the medicine coming up. He said that if it went on the ground that she could not be brought back from the fairies. Cleary asked her was she Bridget Cleary or Bridget Boland, wife of Michael Cleary in the Name of God. He asked her more than once. She answered three times before he was satisfied.'

It seems that Michael Cleary succeeded in forcing at least some of the herbal mixture down his wife's throat. In fact, he managed about three doses of the stuff while his neighbours were there and is said to have made her swallow a further three before they arrived. When this was done, all the men who were present shouted: 'Away with you! Come home Bridget Boland in the Name of God!' Then they clapped their hands and slapped her. However, one of the neighbours who had just come in paid close attention to great burn marks across the invalid's forehead and it was later discovered that she had been threatened with a red-hot poker in order to make her take the herbs. Hearing the voices of the visitors in the kitchen, Bridget screamed loudly. Then Michael Cleary asked his wife again: 'Are you Bridget Boland, wife of Michael Cleary in the Name of God?'. Bridget seemed to make no answer or else her reply was so weak and faint that nobody in the room could actually hear it. Turning to her husband, Jack Dunne said: 'Make a good fire and we will make her answer.'

The fire had already been burning quite well in the open hearth, even though no fuel had been added to it. Gathering around her, the men lifted Bridget bodily from the bed, 'winding' her in the bedclothes, and carried her to the grate. Jack Dunne took her head and James Kennedy her feet, Michael Cleary following with the spoon and saucepan. According to Johanna Burke, Bridget seemed fully conscious and well aware of what was going on. With a little effort, the men held her over the steadily burning flames. With desperation edging his voice, Patrick Boland asked: 'Are you the daughter of Patrick Boland, the wife of Michael Cleary?' Bridget, clearly terrified, struggled a little. 'I am, Dada,' she answered clearly. The men continued to hold her over the flames for at least ten minutes before carrying her back to bed. After subjecting her to this 'ordeal by fire' it may

have been that they felt temporarily convinced that they had
driven the witchlike creature out.

* * *

At about 7.00am on Friday, 15 March, Father Cornelius
Ryan was called from the parochial house at Drangan to visit
Bridget. The priest had actually called on her two days before,
as requested, and was told that she was dying. He had given
her the last rites of the Church, but he refused to come when
called upon that Thursday. Now Michael Cleary turned up at
his door once more and asked him to come. Somewhat reluctantly, Father Ryan did so. He arrived at the house some time
after 8.00 am, said Mass in Bridget's bedroom and gave her
Holy Communion. Bridget, however, was reputed not to
have swallowed the Sacred Host (according to the testimony
given later by her cousin Johanna) but to have surreptitiously
removed it from her mouth with her fingers – something
expressly forbidden by Catholic teaching. If this indeed happened, the action may have sealed her fate because it was well
known that neither witch nor fairy could bear the touch of the
Blessed Host on their tongue. As well as that, both witches
and evildoers often used the Wafer in the preparation of
pishrogues (charms or spells) and in dark magics. Whether
this was communicated to Michael Cleary isn't known but, if
it was, it would have undoubtedly strengthened his belief
about his wife. Father Ryan asked him if he was still giving her
the medicine that Doctor Crean had prescribed but Cleary

said that he had no faith in it. The priest seemed to concur as he spoke of William Crean as being 'always drunk'.

During the afternoon, an argument of some kind appears to have developed between Johanna Burke and Michael Cleary about payment for the milk which the former alleged she had sold to Bridget. According to the evidence given later by Johanna Burke, 'Mrs Cleary asked her husband if I was paid for the milk. I said yes, and showed her the shilling, which she took and put under the blankets and gave it back again in a minute.' This incident later seems to have the source of some trouble between husband and wife, for Michael Cleary withheld milk from Bridget when she asked for it later in the day. It seems that he later accused his wife of having rubbed the shilling on her leg when she put it under the blankets, and interpreted this as a sinister action on her part, as if she was making a spell or 'pishrogue'. The incident also highlights Johanna Burke's possibly ambivalent attitude towards her cousin, of whom she may have disapproved or been jealous.

That evening, some neighbours called to see how Bridget was progressing. In tightly knit country communities this was to be taken as 'good neighbourliness', but they may have been motivated to come by curiosity as well. They sat in the kitchen and later Johanna Burke joined them, making them some stirabout (porridge). Because there were visitors, Cleary got his wife out of bed, had her dressed and brought her in amongst the company. One of the visitors, Tom Smith, asked how she was keeping and she replied that she was 'middling' but that her husband was 'making a fairy of her'. She referred to the fact that her husband would not allow her to drink any of the milk that Johanna had bought and that she had never asked for milk without buying it.

Later that night, Johanna Burke's brothers, Bridget's cousins, Patrick, James and William, arrived back from Michael Cleary's father's wake which had been held in Killenaule eight miles away (Michael Cleary's father had died the day before, but his son had not attended the wake owing, apparently, to his wife's illness). Towards midnight some of the neighbours left, so that now only the immediate members of the family were left — Bridget and her husband, her father Patrick Boland, her aunt Mary Kennedy, her cousins and her cousin Johanna's young daughter Katie. As Bridget was being handed a cup of tea, Michael Cleary got three pieces of bread and jam and insisted that she eat them before she drank the tea. He suddenly asked: 'Are you Bridget Cleary, my wife, in the Name of God?' He asked this three times and she answered him twice, and ate two of the pieces of bread and jam. When she didn't answer a third time, he rose from where he'd been sitting and forced the third piece of bread and jam down her throat, shouting: 'Swallow it! Is it down? Is it down?' He then struck her across the face, flinging her from her seat and onto the earthen floor of the cottage. Desperately, Bridget called on her cousin to intervene — 'Oh Han! Han!' - but Mrs Burke did nothing. Perhaps she was frightened of the violent Michael Cleary who now, in a fit of even greater rage, tore off most of his wife's clothing, leaving her in her chemise in front of the men. Taking a burning stick from the grate, he brandished it in front of her face, as if trying to ram it down her throat. Then, taking the house key, he crossed to the door and turned it in the lock, effectively locking everyone in the cottage.

At this point, clearly terrified by his demented behaviour, Mrs Burke withdrew into the bedroom. Her role in the events, and failure to come to her cousin's aid when she was in mortal danger, seems unclear; perhaps she felt unable to intervene between husband and wife because local propriety forbade that. A few of the others who remained — Johanna's mother, Mrs Kennedy, for instance — had also earlier gone into the bedroom for a bit of a doze. Johanna heard Bridget shout, 'Give me a chance!', then she heard her head strike the floor and heard her scream. The kitchen must have been a scene of total chaos. Michael Cleary was now apparently standing over his wife with the still-burning stick, jerking it at her and threatening her. He jerked it close to her body and it took only a minute for the calico chemise to catch fire.

In the bedroom beyond, Mary Kennedy was hardly more than dozing when she heard her son William cry out from the kitchen: 'Mother! Mother! Bridgie is burned!' She rose up and both she and Johanna Burke shouted, 'What ails ye?' Michael Cleary met them at the bedroom door and with a solemn face turned to Mrs Burke and said, 'I believe she's dead!' Then, walking over to the window, he took down a lamp and, unscrewing a cap, poured paraffin all over the prone body on the floor. There is no doubt that he was now out of control, and as he attempted to set fire to Bridget he was stopped by Mrs Kennedy whom he pushed away. 'What are you doing with the creature?' cried the old woman as she reeled back. 'Is it roasting her you are?' Michael Cleary suddenly darted forward and set fire to his wife's paraffin-soaked body, which was ablaze in an instant. The recklessness of this act was underlined by the fact that he could easily have set the whole house on fire and all of its occupants.

'For the love of God, Michael!' James Kennedy, who had risen from Patrick Boland's bed where he'd been sleeping, had come to the bedroom door and had witnessed the horror. 'Don't burn your wife!' Half-turning, Cleary looked at him blankly. 'She's not my wife', he answered in a low, flat voice. 'She's an old deceiver sent in place of my wife. She's been deceiving me for the last seven or eight days and deceived the priest today too, but she won't deceive me any more. As I beginned with her, I will finish it with her. You'll soon see her go up the chimney!' By this he referred to the traditional escape route for a changeling.

Seeing that the man's wits were clearly gone, William Kennedy, who had come down to the Cleary house with his mother, asked him for the house-key so that they might go, but Cleary only drew a knife and told him that the door wouldn't be opened again until the real Bridget had been returned to him from her imprisonment under Kylenagran-agh Hill. Waving the weapon at William, he threatened to 'run him through' if he attempted to leave. The boy fainted clean away. Turning to the rest of the family, Cleary warned them: 'If you come out any more, I'll roast you as well as her.' Everyone withdrew into the bedroom, leaving Cleary alone with his burning wife. Still holding the lamp, he threw oil on her three times, before sitting down on a chair to watch the flames rise. Some of the others peeped out of the bedroom and Cleary turned towards them shouting: 'You're a dirty set! You'd rather have her with the fairies in Kylenagranagh than have her here with me!'

Patrick Boland came out of the room and informed Cleary that if there was anything that he could do to save his daughter then he would do it. Cleary answered him that he could bury her with her mother who had also been 'of the fairy'. He further told him that next Sunday, he (Cleary) would go to Kylengranagh Fort where the real Bridget would come riding to him on a white horse and that if he could cut the golden straps that bound her to the animal, she would be free and would be his once more. This, apparently, was what 'Ganey over the mountain' had told him, although he would later declare that Bridget had told him it herself. As he spoke, Johanna Burke later told the court, the house filled with smoke and flames crackled around Bridget's body.

Later, under duress, Patrick Kennedy went with Michael Cleary to bury the body at a 'secret spot' nearby, the rest of the family remaining locked in the house by Cleary. Once the body had been buried, Cleary made all who had witnessed the atrocity kneel down and swear on the Holy Name not to reveal it to a soul. He would subsequently tell those who asked that Bridget had simply 'gone away'.

*   *   *

The next day, Saturday, 16 March, Jack Dunne, badly agitated, accompanied Michael Cleary and Michael Kennedy to Drangan village to attend confession in the chapel there. Although Father Ryan was the parish priest — and he seems to have been largely sympathetic towards Michael Cleary, on the surface at least — it was the curate, Father McGrath, who took confession that day. John Dunne went into the box first and spoke quietly to the curate who told him to send Michael Cleary (who was in the chapel yard) in to see him. Cleary came in and, weeping, spoke to Father McGrath, although what was said remains under the seal of the Confessional. The curate, however, deemed that he was 'in no fit state to receive absolution'. He went to fetch Father Ryan and the three of them talked for a long time. All the while, Michael Kennedy remained outside in the chapel yard. Eventually Father Ryan emerged and walked straight across the road and into Drangan police barracks.

Again, nobody knows what was said by the parish priest to Acting Sergeant Patrick Egan inside the barracks, but it was enough to arouse police suspicions. Egan was well known in the locality and he had already probably heard the weird stories that were circulating about Michael Cleary and the mysterious disappearance of his wife. However, he couldn't investigate without a formal complaint being lodged, especially in a tight-knit rural community like Ballyvadlea. Taking another policeman with him, Egan followed Michael Cleary along the Fethard road and, as he stopped at Mary Kennedy's cottage, the policeman approached him and asked him about his wife. Sticking to his original story, Cleary informed him that she had left home 'about twelve o'clock last night' although he hadn't actually seen her going as he had been in bed at the time, asleep (adding that he hadn't slept for about eight nights previously). Egan walked home with him, repeating his questions from time to time. Cleary always answered that Bridget was gone but he didn't know where. As he left the house, Egan heard a distressed Patrick Boland shout from inside, 'My daughter will come back to me!' The old man would insist right up to his trial that his daughter was alive and well and was living 'elsewhere' (with the fairies).

Despite Michael Cleary's assurances, Egan was suspicious and asked for more police from Clonmel to be drafted into Ballyvadlea. Their mission was to look for Bridget. Shortly after these men arrived there was a formal complaint made against Michael Cleary. The name of the complainant has never been disclosed but it is thought to have been William Simpson, long reputed to be Bridget Cleary's lover. Simpson was to claim that Michael Cleary had approached him for the loan of a revolver (which Simpson was known to keep about him) so that he could go up to

Kylenagranagh Fort and 'bring back his wife'. Simpson didn't lend him the gun but he later claimed to have seen Cleary going up the hill carrying a large table knife. Allegedly, Cleary had waited there a long time for Bridget to appear on a white horse, but he had seen nothing.

By now, the situation had become too serious and too complex for the Drangan police station to handle and Patrick Egan passed the case to Inspector Joseph Wansborough in Carrick-on-Suir, who ordered a full-scale search of the area around the Clearys' cottage. Police were soon searching the areas of Drangan, Clooneen and Mullinahone. Wansborough visited a number of homes around Ballyvadlea and took copious notes from those whom he interviewed. He soon obtained his first formal, sworn statement.

It came from William Simpson and was given on Monday 18 March before W. Walker Tennant, Justice of the Peace. Simpson stated that he had witnessed Bridget Cleary being ill-treated in her home on the previous Thursday night. He also named at least some of the people whom he knew to have been there and whom he considered responsible. Once again, police swarmed through the area and those whom Simpson had named were questioned. Johanna Burke went separately to Justice Walker Tennant and swore some further 'information' in front of him, to the effect that Bridget Cleary had left her home while sick and had 'disappeared'. The Justice then asked Wansborough if charges would be brought against anyone. Strangely, given that he now had so much concrete information regarding the case, the first person that Wansborough charged was the slieveen, Denis Ganey. He was charged with 'causing Bridget Cleary to be ill-treated and great actual bodily harm done to her'. This was bizarre since it is supposed that Ganey had never even met Bridget Cleary, even if his influence on events had been profound. All the same, the police net was beginning to tighten around Michael Cleary.

On Friday, 22 March 1895, officers from the Royal Irish Constabulary, guided by William Simpson, searched an area of boggy ground in the area of Tullowcossaun, near to the Cleary home. Away in a corner of a field about a quarter of a mile from the cottage, Sergeant Patrick Rogers of the Mullinahone Constabulary noticed some freshly turned earth and crushed bushes. Constables Somers and O'Callaghan helped him dig down about eighteen inches where they found a dirty sheet wrapped round what seemed to be a woman's body. The corpse itself had been pulled up into a crouching position with the knees almost up against the chin, and the body was very badly burnt. It was naked except for a few remnants of clothing, all badly charred, which had actually been seared into the skin, and a pair of black stockings. The head was covered in a sack and was largely untouched. There was still a gold earring in one of the ears. Tearing away the coarse sacking, Rogers looked at the face and identified it. They had found what remained of Bridget Cleary.

* * *

Now that her body had been found, arrests followed swiftly. Police took a number of people from the Ballyvadlea and Tullowcossaun districts, including Michael Cleary, Patrick Boland, Bridget's father, Mary Kennedy, Johanna Burke, the Kennedy brothers, and Jack Dunne. All across Ireland and far beyond, interest was suddenly focused on a remote area of County Tipperary as the incident became widely known as 'The Clonmel Witch Burning'. Soon obscure Ballyvadlea was known halfway around the world as a place of dark superstition and sinister events. Indeed, elements of the British and Unionist press tried to make political capital of the affair by proclaiming it as evidence of the backwardness of the Irish peasantry and their unfitness for Home Rule.

The defendants were arraigned at the Summer Assizes in Clonmel and were brought to trial on 4 July 1895. The judge, Mr Justice O'Brien, paid scant attention to the talk of fairies and 'witchcraft' and showed little sympathy for Cleary's state of mind at the time. All the same, the talk still persisted and was readily seized on by the press. All this rumour had no effect on Michael Cleary's ultimate sentence — he received twenty years' penal servitude for the manslaughter of his wife.

Jack Dunne and the Kennedy brothers (who had assisted in forcing Ganey's poison down Bridget's throat) were found guilty of 'wounding' — Patrick Kennedy was sentenced to five years imprisonment, Jack Dunne to three, and the other two were sentenced to one year each. Patrick Boland and Michael Kennedy each received a sentence of six months but Mary Kennedy was set free by order of the court. There was some speculation that she had given information which had helped convict the others, but this is far from certain. Early on, her daughter Johanna Burke revoked the first statement she had made to the police and turned Queen's evidence: in the trial she became the chief witness for the prosecution and the evidence she provided was crucial.

From the Assizes at Clonmel, the prisoners were taken to Mountjoy Prison. Jack Dunne was later released on licence and returned to Ballyvadlea. His wife Kate had died and he himself is said to have finished his days as a labouring man, broken and unwilling to talk about the incident. The Kennedys too were released on licence and returned home to work as labourers, refusing to say anything. Michael Cleary, however, remained in prison, being shunted between Mountjoy in Dublin and Maryborough (now Portlaoise) Prison in County Laois. According to some accounts, he learned to work as a tailor and was a rather quiet and withdrawn inmate. He was released on licence from Maryborough on 28 April 1910. It is unclear whether he returned briefly to County Tipperary; some argue that he never returned as 'he couldn't show his face in the countryside'. What is known is that in June of that same year, he boarded a ship bound, via Liverpool, to Montreal and vanished from the pages of recorded history. It is possible that when he arrived in Canada he changed his name and disappeared.

The horrors of the 'Clonmel witch burning' still lie some-where deep in the memories of the people who live in

Ballyvadlea today and there are few in the countryside who are willing to talk about it. The area remains very close-knit and there are descendants of all the main participants in the case living there still. The community, understandably, wishes to consign the whole affair to history. Some vestiges of the Cleary house remain, although the original house itself has long been converted into another dwelling and, as such, is not accessible to the public. Kylenagranagh Hill is still there, of course, but much of the fort which once dominated its crown has been cleared away. It still has a sinister reputation and some old people of the area will tell you privately that the fairies still hold court there on certain nights of the year.

Despite the passage of time, the reticence of local people, and the changes to the countryside, the case still holds a fascination for the general public, perhaps because it happened comparatively recently (just over a century ago) and sporadic tours of the 'Tipperary witch country' continue to be well subscribed, especially by visitors from overseas.

Bridget Cleary seems ultimately to have been the victim of the eerie superstition that ebbed and flowed through the pleasant Tipperary countryside like a black tide. The local schoolchildren still sing an odd and slightly sinister rhyme as they play their skipping games:

'Are you a witch, or are you a fairy,
Are you the wife of Michael Cleary?'

Hedge Witches and Wise Women

Biddy Early

THE WISE WOMAN OF CLARE

The most famous of all the Irish 'hedge witches' is the celebrated Biddy Early who lived near Dromore Hill, near Kilbarron Lake in County Clare. The awe, fear and wonder in which she is held in her native county bubbled briefly to the surface in Frank O'Connor's *Leinster, Munster and Connaught* (1950) in which the writer, railing against the failure of Clare County Council to erect some sort of memorial to the local poet Brian Merriman, dryly observes:

'It is understood that the Clare County Council is proposing to erect a monument to Biddy Early instead. Witches are more in their line.'

Biddy enjoyed her reputed status as Ireland's foremost 'witch' probably because she embodied all the attributes that attended strong-minded, independent women in mid-nineteenth century Ireland. She drank, she smoked, she played cards, she failed to attend Mass, she ignored the priests and, worst of all, when in her old age she took husbands far younger than herself. She was also a 'woman of the people' – a woman who would take part in the rough and tumble of rural life just as a man would do. And of course, she was not afraid to take on the authorities of the day – particularly the Church, which was now trying to adopt a more learned and sophisticated image. As the renowned Biddy Early scholar Edmund Lenihan, himself a Clareman, notes:

'In an era of resurgent Catholicism such as the latter half of the nineteenth century, the church of the majority of Irish people was busily trying to shake off the image of a hole-and-corner organisation, serving the needs of illiterate peasants. The great church-building programme of the mid-century is one of the most public facets of this. Further down the line, at parish level, this resurgence took the form of a desire, among priests in particular, to be seen in a good light by those of a higher social standing. This need not be seen as mere snobbery ... But it could take the form of a narrow authoritarianism, a desire to stamp out all individuality, especially of the kind that might seem to bring unfavourable notice on Catholicism – and such notice was nothing new as can be seen from some of the literature of the time.' (Edmund Lenihan, *In Search of Biddy Early*, 1987.)

Biddy Early represented two strands of society, both of which were repugnant to a Church which was trying to cultivate a sophisticated and urbane image – she was a forthright and strong-willed woman and, moreover, she represented what might be called the 'Irish peasantry' (those without formal learning and supposedly 'cultured' ways about them). For a priest to have a woman such as Biddy within his parish was a diminution of his own status. Small wonder then that she was denounced as a 'witch' from local pulpits and that many locals were discouraged from consulting with her on the pain of endangering their immortal souls. Not that Biddy (or indeed many of her clients) minded – she continued to live her life and practise her alleged skills as before and the stories, both about her and her powers, grew. Some of these stories hinted that she was 'well in' with both fairies and ghosts and that her cottage at Kilbarron contained the impedimenta of evil. Such stories were undoubtedly put about by the clergy and the well-to-do, but they circulated amongst the local country people too and they only added to the aura of mystery that surrounded her.

From her third marriage onwards, Biddy assumed involvement in a new role which we must consider. Her involvement with the peasantry, coupled with her marriage to Tom Flannery, turned her into a quasi-political figure. This was a time of great unrest in County Clare: unpopular laws were in force all across the county with land being doled out to 'foreign landlords' (often men from other counties such as Limerick) and there is no doubt that there was an underground movement amongst the locals to resist this. While there is no evidence that Biddy was directly involved in the disturbances themselves, she probably provided the inspiration that lay behind them and offered through her status as an alleged 'witch' a focus for the discontent that simmered under the surface of Clare society, amongst the common people. These two strands – the opposition of the Clergy and the climate of political unrest – were to add immeasurably to Biddy's legend. Indeed, she was to become the best known of all the Irish 'wise women' and 'witches'. And yet she remains a mysterious and enigmatic figure, wreathed in legend and story. So just who was Biddy Early and did she truly have a shred of the supernatural powers that have been attributed to her across the years?

There is no record of Biddy's birth but she was probably born around 1798 in Lower Faha near Kilanena in Clare. Her father's name is usually given as John Thomas Connor (or Connors), although there are several versions giving him different Christian names, whilst her mother's is consistently recorded as Ellen Early. Whether or not her mother and father were actually married is not known, but from her birth and throughout her long life, Biddy took her mother's maiden surname as opposed to that of her father. Although married at least four times, she was usually known as Bridget Early.

Ellen Early, her mother, was already widely known in the Faha area. There were stories about her stating that when a girl, she had been abducted by fairies and that she had spent some time with them, learning their ways and skills. Consequently, she had obtained knowledge that was well beyond that of ordinary folk and she was regarded as a healer and seeress in her own right. A vague description of her tells of 'a fine looking woman even in her later years' and her apparent youthfulness was attributed to her fairy powers. She was treated with awe and wonder by her neighbours. John Thomas Connor remains something of a shadowy figure but it is clear that he was a labourer, trying to get by on a small farm.

Although Faha is generally given as the site of Biddy's birthplace, as with everything else in her mysterious life there are disputes about this. She was also said to have been born in Carrowroe, a small townland between Gorteen and Moymore in Clare. There is some mention of a 'Bid Connors' (a name by which she may also have been known and which she seems to have disliked) living in the area, but it cannot be said for certain that this was Biddy herself. Other sources give her father's holding as being near Feakle village. No one is really sure.

Nor is there any record of Biddy's early years. Her parents seem to have died when she was still quite young – traditionally this is said to have happened when Biddy was around sixteen years of age. It is not known if Biddy had any brothers or sisters since no mention is made of any other siblings. It is unlikely, although not impossible, that in nineteenth-century Ireland she was an only child. However, in popular legend at least, Biddy seems to have had no siblings worth noting.

What happened to her after the death of her parents is unclear and there are several different versions of events. Some stories speak of her paying rent to various landowners, which seems to suggest that she continued to manage the farm at Faha, just as her parents had done before. How long she did this for is not known. Other tales tell of her immediate eviction following the death of her father (whether her mother was alive at this point is not stated) and of her briefly going to work in a 'House of Industry' (workhouse) in Ennis. What seems to be generally agreed is that by roughly her seventeenth year, she was no longer living at home or working the home tenancy and had been forced to enter domestic service. Again, in the absence of any written record, it is difficult to be certain who she worked for exactly.

One account of her life states that she went directly to Feakle where she obtained employment as a servant with the local doctor – a Dr Dunne who had a large house at Kilbarron. If true, this was her first contact with the Kilbarron area. She didn't actually live in Dunne's house but in a haggard (a small, crude dwelling or outhouse) nearby. Besides the house, the doctor is thought to have owned at least part of a large 150 acre estate on which lived a number of tenants. Whether or not the doctor actually owned the house in which he himself lived is open to question, for he seems to have leased it from some 'oul' gentleman' and employed a number of servants to work there. Until relatively recently, there were those in the Kilbarron area who could point out the direction of 'Biddy Early's haggard'.

As a daughter of the 'fairy woman' Ellen Early, it is said, she soon began to acquire a reputation as a healer around the Kilbarron district. From her haggard, she dispensed what might be described as 'simples' – poultices and healing powders – to those that sought them and in so doing she seems to have supplemented her income as a domestic. There are even some stories of her paying rent for the haggard to Dr. Dunne who is described locally as 'tight-fisted when it came to money', which implies that she was slightly more than a mere servant.

Of course, as with other stories about Biddy, there are those who suggest that this story is false and that Biddy was never employed by Dr Dunne at all. Certain sources say that she left either Faha or the House of Industry in Ennis and went directly to work for a Patrick Malley (or Mally), an elderly widower with a grown-up family who lived in the townland of Gurteenreagh, between Carheen and Ayle. Malley seems to have been relatively rich and although he may not have owned his own farm, he was still wealthy enough to hire servants to work on it and to look after him. Once again, Biddy seems to have lived in a haggard on Malley's property but it was not long before she moved into the farmhouse itself. Later she appears to have moved into the widower's bed as well. Soon she and the old man were married and she became mistress in Carheen — much to the disgust of members of Malley's family, according to some stories.

By this time she was almost twenty and had acquired a strong reputation as a 'wise woman' throughout the countryside. Probably this was due to the fact that she knew about herbs and potions, a skill that she had probably learnt from her mother, and this gave her some standing in the community. This status was enhanced through her marriage to Malley. It looked as if Biddy was set up for life.

And so she might have been had not Malley (an old man at

the time of his marriage) died. There was now a dispute amongst the family as to who should inherit his farm or holding. As his wife, it should fall to Biddy, but then the widower had a number of sons who also had a claim. There was some talk that the family wanted to throw Biddy out and were prepared to go to law to do this. In the end, Biddy solved the problem herself by marrying her eldest stepson, whose name is given as either Patrick or John, and continuing to live on in the house.

For a servant to marry her widowed employer – particularly when he was an old man – must have raised a few eyebrows in the community, but for a woman to marry her own stepson was certainly a scandal. It not only set tongues wagging but drew the disapproving attention of the local clergy. They denounced Biddy, stating that she had put some 'glamour' (charm or spell) on the young man in order to make herself desirable to him. Biddy of course, paid little heed to such censorious denunciations.

As with everything else about her, it's unclear whether Biddy had any children around this time. Some sources state that she had borne a child to the elder Malley and that this was a girl. There are references to young men around Kilbarron 'courting Biddy's daughter' but nothing more specific. If the girl was said to have inherited her mother's magical skills, there is no mention of it. Other accounts disagree and state that Biddy bore a son to the younger Malley but that he was blind and, despite all her great powers, Biddy couldn't cure him. Even here there is disagreement amongst sources, for some stories recount that the blind boy was the son of her third husband Tom Flannery and that he was named Thomas after his father. Several stories state that Biddy's son was a great hurler — inconsistent with the idea that he was blind. All accounts agree, however, that he died while still a relatively young man.

Despite being the butt of local gossip and denunciations from the pulpit, it seemed that Biddy's life was more or less settled. Things were to change though when, to everyone's surprise, the younger Malley died. The family began to round on Biddy once again and a number of accusations were made. In the end, it is said that she left the house and went back to live in the haggard 'due to the spite of the family'. She continued to act as a local 'wise woman' although her situation was now growing increasingly desperate. But there was worse to come.

* * *

The area around Ayle was extremely unsettled and disturbances against local landlords were commonplace. In the district around Carheen a figure whose name is given as Sheedy or Sheehy — a Limerick man — had become the focus of local hatred. It is not altogether clear who he was: according to some accounts, he was a landlord who had bought land in the locality and who was charging high rents to his tenants; others say that he was simply the land-agent for Colonel Westropp-O'Callaghan, who was the landlord, but that Sheehy was lining his own pockets by raising the rents himself. Whatever the truth of the matter, Sheehy was murdered, allegedly by his tenants.

The slaying was a particularly brutal one, reflecting the depth of local anger against the man. It is said that he was either cut to pieces by billhooks or else burned alive in his cottage. In the latter account, rumours circulating in the Ayle area said that the burning sod that had been placed on the thatched roof of his cottage came from the hearth in Biddy Early's haggard. Indeed, there was some speculation, possibly encouraged by the clergy who wished to discredit her and to keep in with the landlords, that the haggard might have been used for the actual plotting of the murder. There was some talk that Sheehy had tried to evict Biddy and that she had refused to go and moreover had cursed him, although this was never proven. One of those taken in for questioning by the Royal Irish Constabulary (RIC) who were investigating the murder was a certain Martin 'Whiskers' Flannery, a senior estate worker on the Westropp-O'Callaghan property. He was an uncle of Biddy's third husband and was said to have frequented her haggard on a number of occasions — probably as one of her 'clients'. This linked the wise woman with the murder in local minds. It soon became evident that Biddy would have to leave Ayle, both for her own safety and to avoid interrogation by the RIC. It is said that she packed up her belongings and set out for Tulla, six miles away, riding on a cart driven by a local man, Johnny Murphy the chair-maker, who helped her move.

Biddy seems to have known Tulla quite well and the story is that she had worked there in former years. She soon got a job there, at Affick House, where she may once previously have been employed as a parlourmaid. At this time, it was owned by a man named Robert Spaight who ran an estate of one hundred Irish acres of land. All this time, her reputation as a healer and soothsayer was increasing, and she was building up quite a clientele around her. People came to Biddy for advice, for healing, to foresee the future and to curse their neighbours. She probably supplemented her undoubtedly meagre servant's wages by charging for her services. Some traditionalists argue that it was around this time that she married the Malleys but others state that she didn't marry at all but had another son — and that this was the blind boy. This tradition holds that he was a great fiddler and that his name was either John or Pat Connors (her father's name).

She came to Tulla around in 1816/17 but how long she stayed there is not known. At some point, however, she seems to have married a certain Tom Flannery who was said to come from either Finely or, more likely, Carrowroe. Tom was a nephew of Martin Flannery who had been detained by the RIC for Sheehy's murder and was reputedly deeply involved in the land disturbances that were afflicting East Clare at the time. Shortly after the marriage, both Biddy and her new husband were on the move again — from Tulla to Kilbarron. The reason for the move is unclear but certain sources say that the marriage and Tom Flannery's connections had aroused renewed RIC interest in Biddy, stirred by the Church and her alleged involvement in Sheehy's murder. In the end, the police investigation into the murder was dropped and no further action was taken against those who had been detained, but by this time Biddy had, in any case, moved on.

She and Tom set up home in a small cottage on the side of Dromore Hill near Kilbarron Lake which rapidly became a shebeen (an illegal drinking house) in which many men of the area gathered of a night. It was supposed to have been a headquarters for local land rioters where attacks on local landowners were plotted. When Biddy died there many years later, it is said that four large cartloads of empty bottles were taken from the premises. The place became a centre for carousing and drinking in the locality with Biddy at the heart of it. She could drink, smoke and play cards as well as any man and over the years her behaviour seems to have become more and more scandalous. Even after Tom Flannery had died, she maintained the shebeen, which always seemed to be full of local labouring men.

Not only this, but Biddy, never very religious at the best of times, had stopped going to Mass. This, coupled with her outrageous and flagrant behaviour, incensed the local clergy. And all the while, her reputation as a healer and a soothsayer was growing. This, of course, led to further allegations from the pulpit that she was a witch and in league with either the fairies or the Devil himself. As Edmund Lenihan heard from an old native of the locality near Tulla:

'Biddy had the name of a bad woman. When we went to school therefore, she was never taught about. We were beaten black an' blue about Brian Merriman an' sure there wasn't much of a difference between his charms an' her doings when 'tis all trotted out.' (Lenihan, *In Search of Biddy Early*)

No description of Biddy would be complete without mention of her blue bottle. This, according to the clergy, truly marked her as a witch and as a servant of Evil Powers. Descriptions of the artifact vary; some say that it was very small, about the size of a medicine bottle, while others state that it was much bigger, about the size of a fortune-teller's crystal ball. All agree that it was made from thick blue glass, too thick to see through but enough to allow strange shapes and patterns to come and go in its depths. How she had actually come by it is uncertain. A story about her says that she received it from a ghost (either the ghost of her dead, blind son who had died when he was very young, or the ghost of Tom Flannery — the variations are often confusing and contradictory), and some say she won it playing cards with a fairy man. In any case, it was the focus of her power. Using this supernatural implement, it was said that she could foresee the future, glimpse events occurring miles away and locate objects either accidentally lost or deliberately hidden. It was even rumoured that she knew the whereabouts of certain hidden treasures. No one but Biddy herself could look into its cloudy, blue depths and come away unaffected. It is said that only one other person ever looked into it – Johnny Murphy, the chair-maker who had helped her move from Ayle to Tulla, and that this had been his price for helping her move (the account is often disputed as it is said that Biddy didn't possess the bottle at the time) and that he was 'never the same afterwards'. The bottle was further supposed to allow the viewer to receive glimpses of the 'Other Country' (the fairy realm), the sight of which could drive humans insane. When consulted, Biddy would sometimes retire and peer into the bottle like a fortune-teller before making her pronouncements. This led to the assertion that she was in direct contact with the 'Other Crowd' (fairies) who revealed secrets to her. All the while, the legends surrounding her grew.

* * *

As the legends grew, so did her reputation. It had now spread well beyond East Clare and Biddy Early, the healer, wise woman and witch was now known as far away as the north of Ireland and in parts of Britain. People travelled long distances to consult her. Invalids journeyed on uncomfortable carts from Belfast to the lonely cottage beside Kilbarron Lake, seeking a cure for their afflictions. Sometimes they obtained one, sometimes they did not. She could choose not to cure them for a number of reasons – they had been to see a priest; she considered the ailment was coming from a domain that was not within her power or that the person concerned had displeased her in some way, either by speaking ill of her or having committed some act against her. And she refused to help those who didn't absolutely believe in her powers. She was always, too, wary of trampling on the province of other so-called witches. Once a man from Kilmurry came to see her with an extremely bad bee sting demanding that she should cure it. 'I can't do a thing for you,' Biddy told him, 'for it was the Coolmeen Lake witch in the shape of a bee that stung you.' Who or what the Coolmeen Lake witch might be, nobody has been able to find out.

Biddy not only cured people but animals as well — indeed a substantial part of her clientele was made up of people consulting her about their animals. In a rural community such as East Clare, animals were very important and the illness or death of one of them could mean destitution for the family concerned. The death of, say, a pig meant that the rent couldn't be paid to the landlord (some yearly rents were paid in the form of a pig) or a disease amongst hens meant that there were no eggs to sell. In the days before vets, animal healers such as Biddy used spells and charms in order to alleviate suffering amongst livestock. It was said that she could cure a sick horse miles distant by uttering some sort of spell over her magic bottle.

As her reputation increased, so did the anger and animosity of the clergy. The longer she continued to draw men to her house and the more she drank and caroused with them, the more she was denounced from the pulpit. Her name was drawn to the attention of the local bishop — his name is often given as Bishop McRedmond — and it is thought that a letter was issued to all priests to read out her name from the altar as a witch and heretic, although whether this was actually done is another matter. This running feud with the clergy led to a famous story about her. A curate from Feakle had stridently denounced her on several occasions and was one day passing the door of her house at Kilbarron. Biddy came to her door, muttered a few words and threw some sort of powder at him that hit the flank of his horse. As he crossed a nearby swift flowing stream, the horse suddenly froze and would neither go forwards nor backwards. The curate had to sit there until Biddy herself came down and released him with a word. This chastened the curate and he never spoke against her again. Other variations of the same story have an aggressive landlord coming to evict her and also being frozen by the power of Biddy's magic until he agreed to let her be.

The continued gatherings in the Kilbarron cottage still attracted the attention of the RIC. The suspicion that she might be associated with local land riots had been strengthened by her marriage to Tom Flannery who was suspected of being a member of a disruptive secret society, and by her continued association with her husband's uncle, Martin Flannery, who was still suspected of being involved in Sheehy's death back in Ayle. She was also suspected of being involved in the illegal manufacture of poteen, which was sold in her shebeen. She was rumoured to be in cahoots with a poteen-maker called 'Mick the Moonlighter' who was said to be one of her relatives. He was evicted and his house razed to the ground. In revenge, he shot the landlord concerned and went on the run. Tom and Martin Flannery were suspected of the murder and were threatened with prosecution in Ennis where Biddy was to be called as a witness. Many people were eager to see the famous 'witch' actually take the stand in court, but they were to be disappointed as the case collapsed when it was found that the real murderer had fled to America. There is also a suggestion (not substantiated) that Biddy was brought to court again in Ennis in 1865, on the insistence of the clergy, and charged under the 1736 Witchcraft Act, but that the case against her was dismissed 'due to lack of sufficient evidence against the accused'. Edmund Lenihan states that she appeared in court (again?) in 1865 charged with witch-craft but there is no record of what the outcome of this was. At this stage, he states, she had married for a fourth time.

It appears that during the time at Kilbarron, Tom Flan-nery had died — Lenihan gives the date of his death as 1840 although Meda Ryan, author of *Biddy Early: Wise Woman of Clare* (Mercier Press, 1978) gives it as 1868 — and Biddy seems to have lost no time in marrying again. Some confusion exists as to the identity of her fourth husband. Generally his name is given as O'Brien from Limerick, although in other accounts his name is given as Thomas Meany (or Meaney) who came from Newcastle West. He came to consult Biddy on a health matter. 'I can certainly cure you,' Biddy told him, 'but only if you'll marry me.' This he did. Tradition also has it that, whatever his name, he was younger than Biddy (who was then in her mid-forties) and that this provoked further shock and outrage in the countryside and incurred the greater wrath of the clergy. It was all very well for an older man to take a young wife, it seems, but not the other way round! She had now been married four times — the longest to Tom Flannery — and some say that even after the death of her fourth husband, she would marry twice more. It is even said that when in her seventies, she married a much younger man of about thirty who preceded her to the grave, causing even greater scandal. There was no doubt, observed the local clergyman in Feakle, Father James Dore, that she had bewitched these unfortunate men into wedlock.

By the late 1850s and early 1860s, Biddy's reputation was known well beyond Irish shores. People were arriving to see her almost by the day, some even from Continental Europe. As with some other 'local witches', there are stories of queues outside her lonely cottage as they waited to be seen. There were other local 'wise women' certainly, scattered across Ireland, but Biddy's fame all but surpassed every one of them. Her main contemporary was a healing woman known only as Mrs Sheridan, who was interviewed by Lady Augusta Gregory at the end of the nineteenth century. An account of their conversation is given in Lady Gregory's *Visions and Beliefs in the West of Ireland*. Lady Gregory gives the only description that we have of her: 'Mrs Sheridan, as I call her, was wrinkled and half blind and had gone barefoot through her lifetime. She was old for she had once met the Gaelic poet Raftrey at a dance and he died before the Famine of '47.' When much younger, Mrs Sheridan claimed that she had been abducted by fairies near Coole in County Sligo and had been taken to one of their halls under a certain hill. It was from this experience that she had obtained her powers and also the ability to see fairy folk. She was famous in her own right as a healer, although not nearly as famous as Biddy Early about whom she would never speak as she didn't believe that Biddy 'did things that were right'. This opinion was held about Biddy by some of Mrs Sheridan's followers. A Mrs McDonagh told Lady Gregory:

'I never went to Biddy Early myself. I think there was a good deal of devilment in the things she did. The priests can do cures as well as she did but they don't like to do them unless they're curates that like to get the money.'

For her part, Biddy never spoke of Mrs Sheridan either and it is almost certain that the two women never met.

* * *

Biddy died at Kilbarron in April 1874 after a brief illness. She had been ailing for some time but her demise was still very sudden. Before she died (and perhaps knowing that she was dying) she decided to make her peace with the Church. She summoned the local curate from Feakle, reputedly a man called Father Fawley, to her bedside and made her confession. She also gave into his keeping the blue bottle, which she kept in a drawer, wrapped in a red shawl. The priest, however, would have no part of such an unholy thing, so on his way back to Feakle he pitched the bottle into Kilbarron Lake. It has never been found since. Ever afterwards, however, it was said that Father Fawley could light candles with the mere touch of his fingers — a power that he had acquired from handling Biddy's bottle!

After her death, her memory lived on, not just in Clare but all across Ireland. She was remembered not only as a witch but as a proud, independent woman, a champion of the poor and an opponent of the domineering clergy and oppressive landlords. These perceptions would add both to her magical status and also to her mystery. She was a strong woman in what was predominantly a man's world. Her life is full of contradictions, nor does it follow any orderly chronology — there are intriguing gaps throughout — and perhaps this too is part of her enduring appeal.

In the mid-1960s efforts were made by a local politician, Dr. Bill Loughnane, to restore Biddy's cottage. He began the work but apparently was dogged by misfortune and the project was abandoned. Today, the name of Biddy Early still resounds around Clare. In fact, a brewery has now been opened, bearing her name! Perhaps Frank O'Connor was right — in Clare witches are sometimes more intriguing than poets.

Moll Anthony

THE WITCH OF THE RED HILLS

Celtic society had a very strong impression of female power. Indeed, many Celtic deities were female and there is no doubt that women played a central role in Celtic community life. Amongst the early Celtic religious leaders were a number of druidesses (or *bandraoithe*) who might be described as female shamans, who were direct conduits to the gods and also custodians of a secret knowledge that lay beyond ordinary mortals. Most of this knowledge was probably about herbs and natural elements and a great number of these women probably acted as healers and midwives. In later years, when the concept of the *bandraoi* had died out, such women often remained as central figures within their respective communities. Those around them still looked to their healing powers and also to their alleged powers of divination – an attribute that had also characterised the druidesses.

Every locality seemed to have its 'wise woman', its 'herb lady' or its 'fairy doctor' – people who seemed to have supernatural skills. But where had these powers and skills come from? For

some – such as those in the Church – there was only one explanation. They came from the Devil and were used to lure good
Christian people into his grasp. Others believed that they came
from the fairies. The link between fairies and wise women was
particularly strong in some areas. In order to keep or renew such
powers, these individuals were in thrall to the Little People. And,
of course, there was a link between the Prince of Evil and the fairies who were his servants, it was said, and who were willing to
lead decent people astray. Even if the Devil were not directly
involved, some wise women and fairy doctors drew their
powers from the darker elements of the surrounding landscape –
from the old powers that dwelt in trees and stone, or in the rivers
and hills. They trafficked with ghosts and sheehogues (unspecified
ancient supernatural forces) whose ways were evil and certainly
not Christian. At least, this was Church teaching on the matter.
According to the Church, those who were involved in such deal-
ings were witches.

Many of these so-called witches dealt directly with the fairies.
In south-west Fermanagh, I myself spoke with an old lady who
recalled a local woman named Ellen Mohan who lived in a
remote and lonely place near Boho and who was consulted by
everyone round about. Each night she would come to the door
of her cottage and bow, three times to the east and three times
to the west, saluting the 'Gentry' as they call the fairies in that part
of the county. If anyone passed her house late at night, my informant told me, it was possible to hear the sounds of merriment

and jollity as if a huge gathering was taking place there. Yet, if the passer-by were to actually call at her door, the sounds would vanish and Ellen Mohan would be sitting there alone. It was widely believed throughout the community that she entertained fairies in her house and in return they granted her powers and knowledge that were well beyond that of any other mortal. Her association with the 'Gentry' made her greatly feared and respected all through the district. There were similar women living in small communities all over Ireland who were supposedly 'well in' with the fairies and other supernatural creatures.

One of the most famous of these women was Moll Anthony of Kildare. Like Biddy Early, accounts of her life are fragmentary and often contradictory but, although not quite so famous as Biddy (who was her contemporary), there is no doubt that she was regarded with a mixture of awe and a little terror by those who lived around her. Her story is difficult to piece together, not least due to the fact that nobody really knows exactly who she was.

One evening, the story goes, a man and a woman were having their evening meal in a small cottage near Punchesgrange, County Kildare, when they were interrupted in the most startling manner. The door of the dwelling opened and four men, all dressed in black, walked in uninvited. They were all tall, pale and grim-faced and not one of them spoke a word. The woman, seated at the table, placed her hand against her mouth to keep from screaming for she and her husband knew quite well that these were the fairy folk and that no good would come from such a visit. The tallest of the men was carrying a box, which looked like a small coffin. Inside it, however, something seemed to be stirring and moving. Walking across to the table wordlessly, he placed the container on its edge and then, without a backward glance, all four men turned and left the room by the way that they had come in. The whole encounter had only lasted for a matter of moments.

Opening the box that the fairies had left, the couple found a small baby girl, wrapped in a red shawl. The child was obviously human; although nobody could guess its origin — the common story was that it was a changeling that, for some unknown reason, the fairies had returned to the mortal world. Efforts were made to try and find the baby's natural parents but all came to naught. Since the couple with whom she had been left were childless themselves, they brought the little girl up as their own daughter. She grew up to become a legendary wise woman and, throughout her long life, she is said to have kept in touch with the fairies that had carried her off. Through this contact, she had great powers — the power of healing, the power of curing sick animals, the power of foretelling the future, the power of finding lost or stolen objects. Her fame spread throughout the county and everybody would know her name, which was Moll Anthony.

The above story is undoubtedly a fiction but it serves to show the mystery and reverence in which Moll Anthony, one of Leinster's most famous healers, was held. There are variations of the same story throughout the province. In one, a boy met a funeral near Punchesgrange, and (as was the custom in those days) he turned and walked a while with the funeral and even carried the coffin. On passing his own house, the funeral stopped and the coffin was placed on the road. The boy ran in to tell his mother but when they came out again, the funeral was gone and the coffin still lay there, now open. Out stepped a twelve-year old girl who gave her name as Mary but had no recollection as to where she had come from. It was deduced that the funeral was a fairy procession and that the girl had been abducted from somewhere else. Nevertheless, the family took her in and she displayed a great knowledge of herbs and cures and was said to have supernatural powers. She grew up to be Moll Anthony.

Some time later, a farmer from County Carlow was drinking in a local pub near Punchesgrange when the girl entered. He recognised her and claimed her as his own daughter who had been taken away by the fairy people many years before and he had not seen her since. Although sceptical, the girl acknowledged that he might be her father but refused to go home with him. Shortly after, she left the family who had raised her and went off to live by herself at the Hill of Grange, County Kildare. This tale connected her directly to the Kildare fairies and, although human, she was said to have been a queen amongst them.

Despite all these tales, nothing concrete is known of Moll's origins or where she was actually born, although it is thought to have been somewhere near Punchesgrange. Traditionally she was referred to as 'the rale oul' Moll Anthony of the Red Hills' but this may be misleading as it is now thought that she didn't live in the Red Hills at all but rather on the bleak Hill of Grange between Milltown and Rathangen. The spot was long considered to be a fairy place and it was said that two fairy paths crossed there, making it an especially magical place. And, just to complicate matters even further, it's also possible that her name was not Moll Anthony at all!

Sir Walter Fitzgerald, the writer and antiquarian who recorded some stories concerning her, suggests that her name was, in fact, Mary Leeson and that she was born in Punchesgrange, although the date of her birth is unknown. However, it is suggested that she was illegitimate and that her birth might have been something of a scandal. Sometime in later life, Fitgerald goes on, she contracted her Christian name from Mary to Moll in order to distinguish herself from other women of the same name living in the area, and took for her surname the Christian name of her alleged father whom he cites as Anthony Dunne, supposedly a labouring man. Thus Moll Anthony was born. If her name actually was Leeson then we don't know whether it was her maiden or her married name, for we don't know whether Moll was married or not. Some say that she married the boy who had seen the fairy funeral pass by his house and who had become something of a 'brother' to her as his family raised her — but nobody is certain. There are frequent references to a son, James, and to a daughter who is named as Mary or sometimes as Catherine. However, it is unclear if these were actually Moll's own children or those of some close relative.

She died, according to Fitzgerald, in 1878, which would have made her the contemporary of the rather more celebrated Biddy Early in Clare. At the time of her death she is described in folktales as 'a very old woman — possibly in her seventies'. It is not clear where she is buried. However, Walter Fitzgerald points to two tombstones in Milltown cemetery.

One of these was erected by a Catherine Leeson to 'the memory of her dearly beloved husband, James Leeson, who departed this life 27 April 1894. Aged 64 years'. James Leeson was always accepted throughout the locality as Moll Anthony's son. If this is the case, then Catherine Leeson, whom many claim was Moll's daughter, might actually be her daughter-in-law. The gravestone beside it is even more enigmatic. The inscription on it reads: 'Erected by Mary Leeson of Punchesgrange in memory of her mother, Eliza Cronley, who departed this life 11 of December 1851, aged 20 years, Also the above named Mary Leeson who died 28 Nov. 1878 aged 71 years'. This, many local people suggest, is the actual grave of Moll Anthony (Mary Leeson) and of her mother Eliza. But Mary Leeson (born in 1807) could not have had a twenty-year old mother who died in 1851. However, on closer inspection, it appears that what looks like the 2 in 20 may actually be a very worn 9 — so Eliza was actually 90 when she died. The evidence certainly seems to suggest that Mary Leeson was Moll Anthony, but we are not completely certain. Mary Leeson, some suggest, was a common name around Punchesgrange and several women bore it around the early to mid-nineteenth century. This may be the grave of some other woman. In the view of Sir Walter Fitzgerald, though, the grave is almost certainly Moll's last resting place.

James Leeson was also said to live on the Hill of Grange. He built a comfortable slated farmhouse on the site where his mother's old mud-walled cabin had once stood. He never seemed to want for anything and is portrayed as a reasonably prosperous farmer. There were some who said that the money that he enjoyed had come from the fees that his mother had charged for curing sick animals but there were also those who said that it came directly from the fairies. There is no doubt that James had a 'cure' for livestock that was said to have been passed down from his mother. But, just to confuse matters even further, there are tales that Moll's cottage might not have stood on the Hill of Grange at all (where James built his house) but on the Hill of Allen. This links her to Irish mythology and heroic tales, for the Hill of Allen was said to be one of the headquarters of the legendary Fianna, the ancient knights of Ireland. It was also the first place to which the hero Oisín returned after his sojourn in Tír-na-nÓg (fairyland). If this was the location of Moll's cabin, then it was said to stand on a fairy path between the Hill of Allen and Donadea's Green Hill along which fairies continually and invisibly came and went. According to tradition, near to her doorway was a stile by which people approached her hut. Uninvited or unwelcome visitors, it was said, were frozen to the spot as soon as they crossed this stile and could not move a muscle until Moll herself came out to release them. This power, it was whispered, came directly from the fairy folk. But this was only one of the tales concerning the wise woman and her relationship with the 'Other Kind'.

*   *   *

It is said that from a very early age, Moll displayed supernatural powers. Whether this came about through a contact with the fairies when an infant or whether, as the Kildare clergy suggested, it was through her worship of the Evil One, is a matter of debate. However, it branded her as a 'special person'. And she had one physical attribute which set her apart. Halfway up her right arm, it was said, she had an oddly shaped, strawberry-coloured birthmark, which never seemed to fade as she grew older. Indeed, it was by this blemish that the farmer from County Carlow who claimed to be her father was said to have recognised her near Punchesgrange, although there were many who said that this was a 'fairy mark', given to her by the Little People. In fact, some said that it had been given to her by the most powerful fairy of all — the Fool of the Forth. The Fool was said to be a being who could bestow great power or take one's wits away simply by a stroke of a rod which he carried – this is the origin of the description for the medical condition of a 'stroke'. The birthmark was supposed to link Moll to the fairy world and might, it was believed, have been at least part of the source of her powers. In rural Ireland, blemishes and minor deformities marked the individual concerned as someone special and apart from the rest of the community. Many so-called 'fairy doctors' were said to have one leg that was slightly shorter than the other.

Moll seems to have begun her magical career, as did many wise women, treating animals around her locality. In the mid-to-late 1800s, there were little or no formal services for the treatment of animals in remote country areas and such services as did exist lay well beyond the means of small farmers. Many relied on the 'cure' provided by the likes of Moll Anthony. And, apparently, Moll had one advantage over a number of other animal healers – she didn't actually have to see or touch the beast in order to cure it. Her word was good enough and she could cure at a distance, no matter how far away.

According to an old tale, a man from the Isle of Man came to Moll Anthony in Kildare one time, and told her that he had a sow that was very sick back at home. He asked her if she could give him something for it – a potion or a powder maybe? Moll Anthony seemed to consider the problem and said a few words under her breath.

'Go home,' she told the man. 'Your sow has recovered but it will not be well for long. Before the month is out, it will be dead and there is nothing more that I can do for it.' And that was the way of it. The man went back to the Isle of Man and found that his sow had indeed recovered but within the month it fell ill again and died. There was nothing that he could do for it. All occurred just as Moll Anthony had said.

Another man away in the North, according to another tale, had a heifer who was ill. 'I'll go to Moll Anthony down in Kildare,' he said. 'You'll not go anywhere near that witch and her Papist charms!' retorted his wife angrily (the man was a Protestant). But he went anyway. When he reached Moll Anthony's hut, she was waiting for him as if she had been expecting his visit. 'You've wasted your journey,' she told him, 'for I can do nothing for you. Your wife cursed me and doubted my powers. The cow will die before you're home.' The man pleaded with her to help him, but to no avail, for Moll seemed to be fixed in her resolve. Sadly he returned to the North and found that all was as she had said. This story was very widespread at a time and was attributed to several other 'wise women' as well, particularly Polly McGarry, a famous animal healer from County Leitrim.

It was not a huge step for Moll to move from curing sick animals to curing sick persons. She was believed to be especially good with fevers and diseases of the stomach and that all she had to do was to touch the person concerned and to say a few words over them and they would be cured, such was her power. And, as with the animals, it was widely reported that she could cure at a distance.

Another tale recounts how two women from County Kerry

went to see Moll Anthony. They left their mother behind near Tralee in the grip of a terrible fever and close to dying. The journey was long and arduous but the two sisters were determined that if there was a 'cure' to be had, they would leave no stone unturned until they had found it. Moll met them coming along the narrow road that led up to her house. When they realised who she was, the sisters climbed down from the cart and pleaded with her to aid their mother. But Moll waved them away.

'There's no need for all this,' she told them. 'I knew of your coming here long ago and I've cured your mother already. She is at home waiting for you and she has baked a cake. But she has lost her ring and if one of you' – and she indicated the sister concerned — 'takes a bit of the cake, she'll find it for it came off her finger in the baking.' The sisters were astonished and returned to Kerry. As they neared their own house their mother, whom they had left dying in her bed, came down to meet them. Shortly after they had gone, she told them, she had started to feel better and the fever seemed to have broken. She was well now — so well that she had baked them a cake. However, she was in some distress as she had lost her ring. One of the sisters cut a piece of the cake and there was the ring in it, just as Moll Anthony had said.

But if Moll could heal, she could also curse. It was said that everyone round about her was afraid to cross her in case she would bring down some sort of awful calamity upon them. And like her healing, Moll's curses could either be applied directly or at a distance.

A neighbour had spoken out against her to the local clergy, runs one anecdote, and Moll got to hear about it, although she was many miles away from the woman. On hearing what was said, she simply spat into the fire. 'There's what I think of her,' she said sharply. 'She'll have no more luck about her than the spittle on the hearth.' And as she spoke, the spittle sizzled and disappeared on the hot stone. 'She'll shrivel up and fade away.' Shortly afterwards, the woman concerned began to waste away and soon she died. This symbolised the extent of Moll Anthony's powers and was a warning to all about speaking out against her.

Another time, a man who lived twenty or so miles from her actually cursed her and Moll cut a stick from the hedge and bent it across her knee. 'See what he makes of that,' she said. The next morning the man concerned awoke to find that his spine had curved, just the same as the rod and he was never able to walk upright again. Such, it was said, was her power.

The clergy in Kildare were not slow to seize upon this aspect of Moll's powers. She was a witch, they declared, acting against God's people. Time after time, so the stories say, she was denounced from the pulpit but, like Biddy Early, she paid this no heed. She was denounced for consorting with the fairies but she paid scant attention to such fulminations. 'If the Little People came to my door,' she said, 'I'd no more turn them away than I would a decent Christian.' Any priest who came to see her usually had to climb over the stile beyond her door and were often transfixed by 'fairy magic' until Moll herself chose to free them. Few of them called twice!

It is said that Moll Anthony died outside the bosom of the Church. However, in the course of her long life, she had made enough money through curing animals, giving out love potions and making charms – it is debatable how much wise women charged for their services but it is known that Moll's powers didn't come cheap to those who sought them – to afford to be buried in a Christian graveyard and with a tomb-stone (an expensive item) on her grave. It seems possible that she was able to leave even more money to her son, enabling him to build his grand farmhouse on the Hill of Grange. How wealthy she was, no one can truly say, but if she had money she did not spend it liberally for by all accounts she continued to live in a small mud-walled cabin.

Like many other 'wise women', Moll Anthony, 'the Kildare witch', remains a hazy and mysterious figure. Nevertheless, this enigmatic woman was undoubtedly part of a tradition that stretched back into the mists of antiquity.

Sorcerers and
Sinister Characters

Alexander Colville

THE DEVIL DOCTOR

One of the fundamental concepts of European witchcraft was the Faustian pact where the witch or warlock sold his or her soul to the Devil in exchange for material gain. This was an extremely prevalent belief amongst Continental Calvinists and was regarded as heresy of the worst and blackest kind. It is the reason why many old women and small children were set on tar-barrels all over the Continent and burned to death – 'for the good of their immortal souls'.

Deals with the Devil began to emerge out of a largely Calvinist Presbyterian canon, although that brand of Presbyterianism was certainly not the only one which subscribed to this belief. But the influence of Presbyterianism in Scotland may have perpetuated the ideology there – Scotland was the only part of the British Isles to treat witchcraft as heresy and burn those who were 'proved' to have been practising it. Those who were the 'enemies of God' were certainly in tangible league with the Devil. And the Devil was close at hand, as far as many Scottish Presbyterians were concerned, temporarily rewarding those who followed him and seeking to lead God's People astray with promises of earthly riches and power. Those who inexplicably prospered, and who led profligate lives, were obviously in league with the Evil One from whom their good fortune derived.

During the seventeenth and eighteenth centuries there was a steady flow of Scots Presbyterians to the north of Ireland. This was especially the case during the 'Killing Times' under the reign of Charles II, when Presbyterianism was counted pretty much as treason against the Crown, and many Scottish Presbyterians fled across the sea to Ulster. Many of those who came were weavers and spinners and, upon arriving in Ulster, they settled along the Province's main river valleys – the Bann, the Lagan and the Braid – where they continued to pursue their trade and founded the basis of the linen industry upon which Ulster was later to depend for its development. With them, they also brought their biblically-based religious beliefs. A good number of these people settled in mid-Antrim close to the Braid River and even today their legacy can still be felt. The prosperous town of Ballymena has always been considered as a bastion of Presbyterianism and this has a bearing on one of the most famous of the Ulster witches, who came from the nearby village of Galgorm: Dr. Alexander Colville.

Galgorm was originally a stronghold of the Mac-Quillans and later of the Scottish MacDonnells, who seized lands from them. A castle there, which the MacQuillans had built, was handed over to a chief of the MacDonnell clan, Colla, who rebuilt it in the Scottish style — a fine, square, box-like layout that it largely retains to this day. Following the defeat of the MacDonnells in the 1560s and the confiscation by the English Crown of the lands they had acquired, James I granted the estates of Galgorm to the English Colville family. Galgorm suddenly changed its name to Mount Colville.

It is highly probable that the Colvilles were not terribly popular landlords. For a start, they were a High Anglican (Church of England) family and they took over just as the area around Galgorm was becoming settled by Presbyterians. The most famous of all the family, however, was the celebrated (or notorious) seventeenth-century cleric, the Reverend Alexander Colville, who was much detested in the countryside round about. Little is known regarding his actual history but his name has certainly become a legend in the district and is still a byword for evil and witchcraft. By all accounts an extremely able and learned scholar, who held a Doctorate in Divinity, he also seems to have been both secretive and aloof, having little to do with his Presbyterian neighbours whom he (as an Anglican minister and member of the High Church) seems to have treated with a mixture of disdain and contempt. They, in turn, regarded him as the next best thing to a Catholic, and appear to have approached him with a mixture of suspicion and revulsion. Not a happy landlord-tenant relationship by any means.

Alexander Colville had been ordained as an Anglican minister in 1622 and had subsequently held the Vicarage of Carnmoney (near Belfast), the Prebend of Carncastle and the Precentorship of Connor. He also possessed considerable wealth, though nobody could say for certain how he had obtained it. Dr Colville's own story was that he had sold land which belonged to his family in England, but there were those who were sure that he had obtained it by means of the Black Arts.

A portrait of Alexander Colville, allegedly painted around 1630, shows him to be a rather portly man with a rather disdainful and arrogant air. This arrogance seems to have infuriated his neighbours, for the Doctor liked to vaunt the supremacy of the Anglican Church above all other religious denominations. Furthermore, he is believed to have been the author of a series of pamphlets on doctrinal subjects, rather pompously dismissing the fundamental beliefs of other Protestant sects when set against his own. His most forthright attack, it seems, was upon Presbyterianism. This was hardly likely to win him the approval or affection of his tenants. He was said to own an extensive library which reflected his enquiring mind and it may be that such a collection included books that it was not considered appropriate for a clergyman to own, or it may be that his Presbyterian neighbours, not altogether impressed by his learned but unimpartial writings, began to attribute certain volumes to his library which were not there at all.

Whatever the reason, stories began to circulate through the community that much of Dr Colville's library was composed of books on witchcraft, devilry and blackest sorcery. It was even said to include a handwritten copy of the infamous *Book of Black Earth* (or the 'Wicked Bible' as the Presbyterians called it) which had allegedly been penned by Alexander Stewart, the Wolf of Badenoch, under the tutelage of a Highland *cailleach* or witch during the fourteenth century; a copy of *The Red Book of Appin* which was so blasphemous that it could only be read by a man whose brow was encircled in a protective band of iron; several extremely ancient works dating back to both Greek and Roman antiquity; and works of the darker medieval scholars. The very names of these iniquitous tomes were anathema to Colville's neighbours and only served to scandalise the people around Galgorm. Indeed, whispers went about that Colville himself was a warlock and that, although a clergyman, he was the Devil's foremost vassal in the north of Ireland. Many claimed to have seen him fishing on the banks of the River Braid (the Doctor was apparently a keen fisherman), surrounded by fairies and evil spirits with whom he seemed to be conversing freely and quite happily.

If the Doctor himself was aware of these rumours concerning his alleged witchcraft, he paid them no heed. However, from time to time, and without warning, he would suddenly raise the rents of the Galgorm estate, much to the annoyance of his tenants who considered him an extremely cruel and tyrannical landlord.

In the late 1630s and early 1640s, according to popular legend, complaints were laid against Doctor Collville by the Presbyterians around him, ranging from ill treatment of his tenants to being a Devil worshipper and leading members of the local community astray with his wicked ways. So seriously were these allegations taken that the Synod of the Presbytery in Belfast commanded the Doctor to appear before it and give an account of himself. Doctor Colville, however, showed the Synod the ultimate contempt by completely ignoring the summons and on the appointed day of his appearance he went fishing instead. This earned him a stern rebuke from the Synod, delivered in his absence, but no further action seems to have been taken against him and Colville chose to ignore the august body's obvious displeasure for he continued much as before.

Stories about him and his diabolical behaviour, however, continued to circulate, all of them incredibly fantastic. It was said, for example, that he roamed the countryside in the form of a giant black and hooded crow, spying upon his neighbours and finding out ways in which he could either bully or blackmail them to his will. He was also said to travel through his lands invisibly, stealing from even the poorest of his tenants, when he could, so that they could not afford to pay their rents and he could then turn them out. He was reputed to have a magic mirror somewhere in the depths of the castle in which he could witness and influence events that were happening in faraway places, even in the Royal Court in distant London. It was further said that he commanded legions of dark and evil spirits who brought sickness, misfortune and even death to the countryside all around Galgorm and many miles beyond. There seemed to be no blasphemy or depravity of which he was not capable, according to rumours.

The most famous tale concerning Doctor Colville, one that is still repeated even today, is that he sold his soul to the Devil. As recently as a few months ago, I myself personally spoke to a man in the village of Cloughmills, not far from Galgorm, who told me of 'an oul' doctor' (he didn't mention Colville by name) who had been visited by 'a black dog that was the Devil' and of how he had given the diabolical animal his soul. The old man told me that it was 'a famous story' in the district and that he had heard it both from his father and his father's father. He also mentioned that a good number of local people were still afraid to go past the ruined church of Galgorm Castle after nightfall for fear of meeting either 'the oul' doctor' or the Devil himself. He also mentioned that some people had seen Colville's ghost in the castle grounds, 'even in the middle of the day an' when it was very clear'.

The story of Doctor Colville and the Devil bears more than a passing resemblance to a number of other diabolical tales in which a cunning mortal sorcerer tries to cheat the Enemy of All Mankind out of carrying off his soul whilst at the same time obtaining great wealth for himself by means of an Infernal Pact. It is possible that the tale originated else-where and was ascribed to the Doctor by the Presbyterians who loathed him. However, it has marked Doctor Colville out as one of the most famous 'witches' of the north of Ireland. With some variations (depending on the teller of the tale), the story of Colville's diabolic pact is as follows.

* * *

Despite being a clergyman, Dr Colville was extremely fond of gambling and of good living and he soon frittered away the fortune that he had inherited at the gaming table and on expensive luxuries. Consequently, he was soon bankrupt and, having nothing left to barter with, he resolved to use his dark powers to replenish his financial reserves. This entailed a plan to sell his soul to the Devil in exchange for gold. Now, the Doctor was shrewd enough to realise that his spirit, stained and corrupt through years of hedonistic living as it was, would be of very little value to the Evil One. Satan certainly placed a high value on the souls of ministers and of godly men, but the shabby shade of a rascally Episcopalian clergyman was unlikely to be of much interest to him. Dr Colville was, nevertheless, a wily old reprobate and he had a plan in the back of his mind by which he could cheat the Devil. Taking down one of the great ironbound books from his 'infernal' library, he performed the appropriate rituals and uttered the appropriate incantations to make the Evil One appear before him. Within a moment and in a reek of sulphurous smoke, the Eternal Enemy was standing in the sorcerer's secret chamber in Galgorm Castle. If Dr Colville had been expecting a shaggy monster with horns and infernally glowing eyes, he was very mistaken for the Prince of Darkness appeared as a small, pallid, clerical-looking man, dressed entirely in black, peering at his summoner over an old-fashioned pair of half-moon spectacles perched on the end of his long and pointed nose. Indeed, he looked more like a lawyer or a Presbyterian minister than the Father of All Lies. Under his arm was a large leather-bound ledger in which he recorded all those souls that were damned.

'Well?' he demanded irritably and in the thin, pinched voice of a clerk, 'why have you disturbed me when I'm extremely busy counting the souls that I've harvested for myself across the year?' The Doctor told him of his proposal – namely, the sale of the soul for an agreed sum. Opening the ledger, the Devil scanned the pages closely, running an ink-stained finger down the lines until he found Dr Colville's name. Looking up, he adjusted his spectacles and gave the anticipated response.

'My dear sir, all souls are of interest to me,' he began smoothly and with a thin smile. 'But you must realise that some are worth more than others. I'm sure that a man of your undoubted education will appreciate such a distinction. Some are fresh and unblemished – those of maidens, saintly men and tiny children for example – whilst some are so stained and filthy with inherent evil and with the corruption of the world as to be almost worthless. I'm afraid, my dear Dr Colville, that yours lies in the latter category and, whilst I'm certainly prepared to negotiate a deal with you, I'm afraid the price which your soul will fetch will not be very high.' And he laughed a trifle unpleasantly. Seemingly unfazed, the Doctor simply gave a wintry smile and replied that, as he was in dire financial straits and with creditors pressing him, he was prepared to accept a relatively low figure for the surrender of his soul — indeed, he was prepared to take the payment in two instalments if need be. All that the Devil had to do was to fill an old top boot (a riding boot that covered most of the leg) with gold and then an ancient soft hat that the Doctor kept about him with the same. Dr Colville would be well satisfied and the Devil could have the soul. The actual date for the surrender of the spirit, the Doctor suggested, should take place twenty years hence on 25 December.

The Devil, however, suspected some sort of trick since 25 December was, of course, Christmas Day, the birthday of the Saviour Jesus Christ, when, traditionally, he had no power and couldn't claim his bargain. After some thought, the Master of Lies suggested that the date of the surrender should be on the last day of February, twenty years hence, and after some haggling and minor adjustments to the time, this was finally agreed. Producing an agreement from somewhere under his coat, the Devil instructed Dr Colville to sign, which Colville did readily (in some versions of the story, he signs it in his own blood which the Devil draws from his thumb). Under the terms of the agreement, the Doctor was to receive the first instalment of the payment right away and the second in seven years' time. After twenty years had elapsed, his soul would be the Devil's to claim.

The Devil then requested to be taken to the Doctor's top boot, which was to be filled with golden coin as specified. The stiff old boot was standing upright against a wall in the scullery of the kitchen, as though waiting for the requested coin, and Dr Colville insisted that the Evil One fill it to the top straight-away. Laying down his ledger, the Devil snapped his fingers, causing a shower of twinkling coin to fall into the gaping mouth of the old boot and instructing it not to stop until the boot was completely filled. This took some time — far longer than could be expected. The gold continued to flow, but the level of the money in the boot never seemed to increase, much to the Devil's amazement.

There was a good reason for this as what Satan didn't know was that it stood over a large hole in the floor of the scullery which led directly to the cellars of Galgorm Castle, and that the wily Doctor had cut away its heel, allowing the shower of golden coins to tumble down into the vaults where his servants were shovelling it into great piles. Too late, the Devil realised that he'd been tricked, but he was bound by his word and there was nothing that he could do about it. He had to fill the old boot up to the top and so he had to stand by and watch as the gold poured endlessly into the cellars below. At length the vaults were full to bursting and the old top boot itself was full, as had been stipu-lated. With an angry howl, the Devil disappeared in another puff of reeking smoke, promising that he would have his vengeance in seven years' time. Dr Colville merely smiled, stating that he would look forward to their next meeting.

For seven further years, Dr Colville was said to have lived at Galgorm Castle in the lap of luxury. He wanted for nothing and spent money lavishly. However, his previous disposition towards his tenants did not improve in the slightest with his newfound wealth, for he was still as cruel and heartless as ever. He continued to evict many of them from their cottages and to confiscate their lands for his own purposes and he continued to use the Black Arts against those who crossed him.

At the end of seven years, the Devil came again as agreed. Fearing another trick, the Infernal One refused to meet the Doctor at Galgorm Castle and so their meeting place was an old limekiln that lay mid-way between Galgorm and the neighbouring village of Broughshane. This time, Satan appeared in the guise of a tall, muscular, ferocious-looking blacksmith with a leather apron, his face and body covered with soot and smuts from the forge. In his right hand, he carried a mighty hammer, which he menacingly swung to and fro. The Doctor, however, was not put off by his appearance and was already waiting for him by the very edge of the kiln, with his old, soft felt hat outstretched. This he required Lucifer to fill to the brim, just as he had with the old top boot.

With a snap of his fingers, the Devil caused another shower of gold coin to fall into the hat. Despite his precautions, however, he found that he'd been cheated by the Doctor once more for there was a thin slit in the crown of the hat and the gold poured right through it and into the kiln below. Bound by his oath, Satan could not stop the flow of gold until the hat was filled and once again this took some time and was extremely expensive because the kiln was very deep. Again, Satan departed with a snarl, promising that the last laugh would be his when he collected the Doctor's soul at the end of thirteen years. Dr Colville, however, had other ideas.

He continued to live like a lord, even going so far as to extend the castle and making great improvements here and there. He added, for example, a walled garden, a sundial and splendid walkways to the demesne. He extensively increased his wardrobe and was never seen attired in anything but the smartest clothes. He bought the finest food and the best wines and brandies with which he gorged his already portly frame. All the while, his tenants went ragged and hungry and, although he was a churchman, not a morsel did he give them. He truly could be considered as a godless man.

However, as the end of the twenty-year agreement drew closer, people noticed that Dr Colville was becoming slightly more pious in his ways. Not that it seemed to do him any good – he would seem holy for a little while but would soon revert back to his old reprobate ways. At the end of the agreed period, the Devil came for his soul. This time, he came as a tall dark-skinned man, wrapped in a green travelling cloak. When he arrived at Galgorm Castle, he found the Doctor within the old church, the ruins of which still stand beside the castle itself. The so-called clergyman was apparently engrossed in reading from the Bible by the light of a single flickering candle placed on the end of a pew beside him. In a booming voice, the Devil commanded him to rise and accompany him to Hell where a particular place had been prepared for him.

'Just a moment,' Doctor Colville raised a restraining hand. 'Let me finish this portion of Holy Scripture before I am taken. Promise me that you'll wait until this small candle burns down so that I can continue to read God's Holy Scripture until it is time to depart.' Somewhat reluctantly, the Devil gave his agreement. In fact, he could do little else for it is well known that no ghost or evil thing can approach a man whilst he is reading God's Word. With a loud cry of triumph, Dr Colville snuffed out the candle with his finger and thumb and placed it between the pages of the great ironbound Bible in front of him, slamming it shut. 'Then it will never be completely burned down,' he shouted, his voice echoing around the ancient church, 'it will never be lit again! Nor can you take it from among the sacred pages.' This was true, for the Devil couldn't open the Bible and take the candle out to light it. Once again the wily Doctor had outwitted him and he was forced to vanish in another puff of reeking smoke, leaving Colville behind.

* * *

From this point, there are two distinct versions of the tale. For example, in his book *Irish Witchcraft and Demonology* (1913), the Reverend St John Seymour states that the Bible and candle were buried with Dr Colville in his tomb at Galgorm. This version was also told to me by the old man in Clough-mills who refused to go anywhere near the tomb which lies within the ruined church. However, another, more persistent version states that the candle-stump was later completely burned down by an elderly maidservant who was doing some cleaning in the Doctor's study while he was away. It was a dark winter's evening and the Doctor was seeing friends in Belfast. The old woman entered the chamber and, confused by the long shadows and poor light, looked around for some form of illumination. The Doctor had left the great Bible open on his table and turning through it, the old servant came on the candle-stump, which seemed the answer to her problem.

'He'll not mind me having this wee bit o' light on such a dark evening,' she said, lighting it. As soon as it had completely burnt down, a demonic laugh followed by a sound like a clap of thunder echoed through the castle. When Doctor Colville returned from Belfast and heard what had happened, he turned pale and started to tremble violently.

'You've condemned my soul to Hell,' he told the old woman as he dismissed her from his service. However, the Doctor was still a very resourceful man and was determined not to be outdone by Satan. Soon he had devised a plan to deal with the situation. From that day onwards, every year as the end of February (the last day of February being the date agreed for the collection of the soul) approached, Dr Colville would gradually become more and more pious. The rest of the year would be spent carousing and gambling but, for the latter half of that month, Dr Colville would devote his time to prayer, singing religious psalms or reading from God's Word. This was designed to keep away the Devil until the first of March, when Dr Colville would resume his old ways again and become as bawdy and heartless as ever – until, of course, the middle of the following February.

Finally, when one 28· February had passed and the great clock in the hall of Galgorm Castle had just struck midnight, Dr Colville laid aside his religious books and climbed the stairs to one of the upper rooms where some friends were gathered for an evening of wagering and drinking. Lifting a glass of brandy, he raised it in a toast to his company.

'A good swallow of brandy, a good game of cards with my friends,' he said. 'I declare this is the best first of March that I've ever spent!' His companions looked at him in astonishment.

'But it's not the first of March yet!' said Mr. Spence from Broughshane who was sitting just across the table from him and who always kept an almanac close by him. 'It's the 29th of February – this is a leap year!' At this, the Doctor turned very white and dropped his glass.

'What?' he stammered. 'A leap year? It can't be!' And he glanced around fearfully for his Bible. Where had he put it?

By then it was too late anyway, for there was a hammering on the door of Galgorm Castle that echoed through the building like the rumble of thunder. When an old manservant opened it, there stood a tall dark-skinned man in a green travelling cloak. Ignoring the servant's protests, he strode into the castle and up the stairs to the room where the Doctor was cowering. 'It's time that our bargain was completed, Dr Colville!' he boomed in a deep and hateful voice. The Doctor started to protest, imploring that there must be some sort of compromise but, without a further word, the dark man threw out his travelling cloak, wrapping it around the cleric, and the pair of them vanished from the middle of the room and before the eyes of the astonished guests, in a whiff of foul-smelling smoke. Neither was ever seen again.

But if such a story is true, say the doubters, then who lies in the dark, underground tomb in the now ruined Galgorm church beside the castle? The church is a black and forbidding place, even on the brightest of days. The tomb itself is accessed by a flight of worn steps, which lead down under a low arch to a subterranean chamber beneath the high altar of the ruin. The darkness within is almost total and it is here that Alexander Colville is supposed to lie in the farthest corner. My informant from Cloughmills told me that he was placed in seven coffins to contain his great evil – each coffin placed inside the other in the manner of a Russian doll. Over the years, he said, the outer coffins have all decayed and worn away 'but the last one is made out of lead and lead can always keep evil in'. Maybe, even in death, the influence of the evil Doctor still lingers there.

* * *

Although not so widely told now, the story of Dr Colville and the Devil was once known throughout Ireland and was reputedly used by the novelist J. Sheridan Le Fanu as the basis for his celebrated and frequently anthologised ghost story *Sir Dominick's Bargain*, in which a local landowner cheats Satan but makes exactly the same mistake regarding the date as the Doctor, and consequently suffers a similar awful fate. In fact, Sir Dominick Sarsfield, the main protagonist of the story, is said to have been based upon the persona of Dr Colville himself.

Following the Doctor's death, the Galgorm estate subsequently passed into the hands of the Mountcashel family through the marriage of his great-granddaughter to Stephen Moore, the first Baron Kilworth and Viscount Mountcashel. Colville's name, however, lived on in the district, firmly associated with evil and witchcraft, a tribute to the hatred and suspicion with which he was regarded during his lifetime.

And perhaps there might have been something to his sinister reputation, for it seems to have flourished even beyond the shores of Ireland. Some time later, shortly after Dr Colville's death, according to Robert Law's *Memorialls*, a maidservant in the employ of Major-General Montgomerie of Irvine in Scotland was brought to court on a charge of stealing some silverware from her employer. Whilst admitting the theft, she defended herself by declaring that she had been forced to do this through raising the Devil by witchcraft. She then went on to give a fairly detailed account of the methods employed to raise the Evil One that shocked everyone present by their explicitness. The examining magistrate asked the girl where she had learned such blasphemies and such abominable witchcraft, to which she replied that she had been taught that particular branch of the dark arts when formerly employed in Ireland, at the house of a certain Dr Colville 'who had habitually practised it'.

Today Galgorm Castle is owned by the Brooke family. The garden which Dr Colville himself laid out, with its sundial and pleasant walkways, is also still there. Local people still state that his ghost can be seen there consulting the old dial at certain times of the year. The Doctor's portrait hangs in the castle's main hall and a widely-held tradition has it that if it is ever removed, for any reason, then some terrible calamity will immediately befall both Galgorm Castle and the village nearby. Many people are still afraid to cross the grounds of the place late in the evening. Stretching down through the centuries, the long shadow of Alexander Colville, be he malignant warlock or much vilified Anglican minister, moves through the mid-Antrim countryside like some ghastly blight, even in these apparently more enlightened times.

Some Minor Irish Witches and Wizards

Although, as we have seen, witchcraft trials were few and far between in Ireland, the names of several famous witches and wise women have come down to posterity – Dame Alice Kyteler, Florence Newton, Biddy Early. Coupled with the names of these famous sorcerers are references to others who are maybe not so well known but who have become a part of rural folklore. Today only their names survive – Peggy (or Polly) McGarry of County Leitrim; Old Deruane from Inishmaan; John Fagan of Connemara; Margaret Docherty of Clonmany in County Donegal – and virtually nothing is known about them. Even these names are fast fading from the communal memory.

Some details regarding certain of the more obscure 'wizards, witches and wise women', however, are known. Much of this detail is not widely available outside their own localities but, nevertheless, contributes to the overall picture of Irish witchcraft.

Perhaps the most famous of these relatively minor sorcerers was Gerald Fitzgerald, the sixteenth Earl of Desmond and Kildare, widely known throughout County Limerick as 'the Wizard Earl', killed in battle with the English in November 1583. Indeed, so much a part of local folklore has he become that he is said never to have died but to be living beneath the waters of Lough Gur in an enchanted castle. Every seven years, according to popular legend, he reappears briefly in the mortal world (usually about May Eve or Hallowe'en) and can take back to his underwater stronghold, if he so chooses, the most beautiful girl, or the strongest man, or the greatest scholar in the district.

A legend states that the earl did indeed dwell in a castle on an island in the middle of the lake, where he conducted strange experiments and fearful sorceries and where the Devil is said to have visited him on several occasions, travelling in a coach made from human bone. The island was linked to the mainland by means of a narrow causeway over which only guests whom the earl wished to see could pass. Most of his diabolic work was conducted in one of the turret rooms, which he maintained as a laboratory, filled with the impedimenta of vilest witchcraft. It was said to contain potions and powders which could transform human beings into animals, crystals that could summon demons and a mirror in which the earl could see all across this world and into the other world beyond.

The Earl of Desmond took a wife, the legend continues,

and brought her home to live with him in his castle at Lough Gur. She had the entire run of the building except for the closed turret room, which housed his Satanic laboratory. He is said to have kept the door of this room locked and had placed a spell about it so that persons seeking it would wander the corridors and never find it. The girl, of course, was curious, especially as he shut himself away there on most nights and she pleaded with him to show her what went on there. At first the earl refused, but she prevailed upon him time and time again until at last he agreed. The agreement was made on one condition, that no matter what horrors she saw in the room she must not cry out or make the slightest sound. This she agreed to and so the earl took her up to his turret room. Here, she saw horrors beyond imagining as the earl transformed himself into various hideous shapes and summoned up a number of foul and disfigured entities. And through all this, the girl bit her lip and clenched her fists until the blood ran but never a sound did she utter. As horror piled on horror, the situation became too much for her and, opening her mouth, she finally emitted a long and terrified scream. At the sound, there was a clap of thunder, lightning struck the turret and the waters of Lough Gur rose up and swallowed the island and its castle entirely.

However, this was not to be the end of the tale for, up until the twentieth century, many people still claimed to have seen the 'Wizard Earl' walking along the shores of the lough, either in the very early morning or late afternoon.

The vision was a portent of great evil and in many cases the earl tried to inveigle the person away with him, presumably to his lair under the lake. One such story appears in the work of the noted Irish writer, J. Sheridan Le Fanu, who knew the area around Lough Gur well and was friendly with the Miss Baileys (particularly Miss Alice Bailey) who then owned these lands. He records how he had interviewed an old servant, Moll Rail, who told him how as a young girl (at the time of interview she was a very old woman) she had met the earl one morning as she was washing clothes by the loughshore. He had spoken to her very kindly and she, assuming him to be one of the gentry who was staying with the Miss Baileys, answered him courteously. He offered her a golden ring if she would come away with him and, flattered by his attention, she agreed to do so but wished to finish washing the clothes. He placed the ring on a nearby rock but it fell off into the lough water, where it turned to circles of blood and disappeared. Moll Rail then knew who the handsome man was and crossed herself, whereupon the earl promptly vanished. Even as an old woman, Moll maintained that she still clearly remembered the incident and was able to give Le Fanu a vivid description of his apparition.

In other accounts, the earl rides a great white horse around the shores of the lough at midnight and serves as a portent of doom to all who meet him. A similar account to that of Moll Rail concerns a blacksmith, Teigue O'Neill, who shod the earl's horse, mistaking him once again for a great noble, only to realise his mistake when he inadvertently uttered the name of God and the earl disappeared. In another account, he appears at the fair in Knockaney and sells a bewitched horse to another gentleman. The local stories and legends surrounding the 'Wizard Earl' are legion and have long formed a part of the folklore of the district.

It is quite possible that Gerald Fitzgerald did indeed dabble in the 'occult arts' – in fact it is quite possible that he was an alchemist, or early scientist. He was known to have a lively and enquiring mind and seemingly took an interest in some of the sciences, particularly early chemistry. This facet of his character was undoubtedly used against him by his enemies – both the English themselves and the English-backed Butlers, the Dukes of Ormond, who vied with the Fitzgeralds for power and lands in the Irish midlands. As with the 'wise woman', then, the alchemist/scientist becomes transformed into the fearsome magician and the tales of the 'Wizard Earl' and his occult activities are actually probably little more than anti-Fitzgerald propaganda.

* * *

The Fitzgeralds also feature in some other Limerick witchcraft legends. The protagonist this time is not a great earl or noble but a nun.

The remains of St Katherine's Augustinian Convent at Shanagolden, known locally as 'The Old Abbey', are now fearfully overgrown and are almost impenetrable to the curious visitor. Little is known about the abbey itself – when it was founded, or even the exact names of some of its abbesses. The first mention of it is by an Inquisition of 1298, enquiring into land entitlements. The ruin still exudes a palpable air of menace and is widely reputed to be haunted. Shanagolden also enjoys another, equally sinister, reputation – it is one of the very few holy houses that had to be closed on the express orders of a pope.

In 1640, affairs at the abbey were brought to the attention of the papal authorities. At the centre of these goings-on was a certain abbess who remains nameless (Westrop and Wardell, writing in the *Irish Archaeological Journal*, simply refer to her as 'a woman of the Fitzgeralds') but who was known locally as 'the Black Hag'. It was alleged that, under her guidance and supervision, the nuns at St Katherine's were turning to witchcraft and blackest sorcery. Few details of what went on are known but it is thought that the abominations included the worship of Lucifer within the convent. It is also suggested that several of the nuns were 'possessed', perhaps in the manner of the nuns of Loudon in France who were said to be possessed by the devil. Tradition has it that the matter was brought directly to the attention of the Pope, Urban VIII, who was a formidable opponent of witchcraft and sorcery. He ordered the convent to be dissolved and the nuns reallocated to other holy institutions. All, that is, except for the abbess, who was considered 'too corrupt and defiled' to be taken in elsewhere. Whether this was indeed the case or whether the abbess herself refused to leave Shanagolden is unknown. The Pope also ordered that all records and impedimenta taken from the place were to be destroyed or else locked away from human view. Of course, many of the stories concerning the closure of St Katherine's may be due to a general Anglican anti-Catholic propaganda which was circulating in both England and Ireland around the time of the dissolution of the monasteries and for many years afterwards.

The abbess went on living at Shanagolden and, by all accounts, continued with her witchcraft practices. Indeed, she reputedly became one of the foremost practitioners of the 'vile art' in the district. However, she also seems to have been something of a recluse, living in the convent sacristy and hiding away when strangers came by. According to tradition, she still wore a ragged nun's habit and her face had become so dirty on account of her never washing, that the skin had actually turned black with grime, giving her the nickname of 'the Black Hag'.

She was widely known as a 'cup tosser' – one who could tell the future by 'reading' the residue in a cup or goblet (today there are people who still claim to be able to predict the future by studying tea leaves in the bottom of a cup) and a herbalist. It must have been exceptionally frightening for local people to see such a creature out in the meadows around the now-abandoned abbey, dressed in a dark and torn habit, gathering herbs in the late evening. Furthermore, the times in Ireland were extremely unsettled and it was said that no great lord of the area would make war on his neighbour without consulting the Black Hag first. This contributed greatly to her reputation as a witch and a sorceress.

No date is given for the abbess's death but local tradition claims that she was found one morning sitting in a chair in the sacristy by a passing pedlar. She was stone dead and there was a look of horror on her face which is said to have greatly terrified the poor man. It was said that the Devil had eventually come for her evil soul. There is no traceable account of her burial. Since then, the convent has gradually slipped into obscurity (perhaps due to the confiscation of its records by the papacy and confusion with another holy house also dedicated to St Katherine), becoming a haven for local raparees (or outlaws), and today it is simply an overgrown ruin. The sacristy or 'the Black Hag's Cell', as it became known, is still there but it is now all overgrown. The legend of the Black Hag of Shanagolden, the 'woman of the Fitzgeralds', however, is still remembered by some old people in that part of the country.

Another Fitzgerald lady who bore a slight taint of witchcraft was Katherine Fizgerald, widely known as the Old Countess of Desmond. The allegations seem to have arisen out of the countess's great age — it is said that when she died, she was a little over 140 years old! Although there is no way in which we can verify that she actually lived to such an extraordinarily great age, her dates are normally given as c.1464-1604 and she claimed to have danced as a young girl with King Richard III and to have been kissed on the cheek when an old woman by Sir Walter Raleigh.

In an age when life expectancy was much shorter than it is today, her great age drew many comments — it was regarded as a wonder of the time and there were hints that the countess had obtained her considerable longevity through a deal with the Devil or by practising 'foul sciences'. There is most probably no substance to any of these rumours. Like the 'Wizard Earl', the 'Old Countess' was said to have a lively and enquiring mind and her interest in the world around her, coupled with an active lifestyle, was more probably the secret of her advanced years than any witchcraft practices. However, more than likely, it suited the enemies of the Fitzgeralds to tar her with the brush of sorcery.

* * *

If the Fitzgeralds suffered at the hands of the rumourmongers, so did the O'Briens of County Clare. They had once been kings and princes of Thomond but when their territory was turned into shire-lands during the English Plantation in the late 1500s (County Clare was created out of the old kingdom of Thomond at this time), they found themselves largely reduced to the status of tenants in places that they had once owned.

The most formidable and celebrated of all the O'Brien women was the seventeenth-century matriarch, Máire Rua (Red Mary) of Leamaneh Castle. Although Leamaneh was her main stronghold, there are stumps of other castles scattered throughout County Clare that are reputedly associated with her. And in many parts of the county she is widely regarded as a 'witch woman' who used her magic to bring power to both herself and her family. She is usually depicted as a proud and arrogant woman who used both sorcery and her female wiles to cling onto wealth and influence.

She was actually born into affluence at Bunratty Castle, County Limerick, in 1615. She already had royal blood in her veins, as her mother was the daughter of the third Earl of Thomond, descended from the old O'Brien kings, whilst her father was Turlough (Turloch) McMahon, Lord of Clonderlaw, a barony that lay between Kilrush and Kildysart in present-day County Clare. She had originally been married, at about fifteen years old, to Daniel Neylon, a wealthy landowner. He unfortunately died when Máire was only in her early twenties, leaving her with four children but with ownership of an estate in Dysert O'Dea, in North Clare.

As an important landowner, she was much sought after as a wife by many of the Clare aristocracy. However, when she eventually did marry again, she married for love – this time to one of her own cousins, Conor O'Brien, who held lands at Leamaneh on the edge of the Burren. There were whispers that she had used spells and charms to cause her cousin to fall in love with her, and even though the couple seemed remarkably happy, rumours of Máire's sorcery still persisted. For instance, it was said that she had poisoned her first husband in order to receive his lands and that she used witchcraft against her enemies. There is no doubt that Máire Rua was a proud and haughty woman who had made her own way in a largely masculine world and that her success had made her many enemies. She was also seen as very greedy and no matter how much power, land and money she acquired, she still wanted more. Given this background, she was certainly a suitable target for accusations of witchcraft.

By the late 1640s and early 1650s, the political situation in Ireland changed as the Cromwellian plantation took hold. Probably motivated by greed, the opportunistic O'Briens rode out, attacking incoming English settlers with a view to driving them off their lands, which the O'Briens themselves then seized. Some of these attacks were allegedly led by Máire Rua herself and no matter how often the English fought back, she always seemed to escape – adding to her already fearsome reputation as a sorceress. As she was such a formidable woman, she had many enemies, most of whom were happy to perpetuate the witchcraft legend. Her husband, Conor, however, was not so fortunate and was shot dead during an attack on Leamaneh itself. After a twelve-year marriage, Máire Rua was a widow once more. She took command of the forces, fighting a guerrilla war against the incoming English, but her cause was already failing.

Two years after Conor's death, Leamaneh Castle was once more besieged as the Cromwellian forces tightened their grip on the country and crushed all rebellions. Realising that there was no way in which she could now hold out and that her cause was lost, Máire Rua demanded to see General Henry

Ireton, Cromwell's commander in Ireland (and the Lord Protector's son-in-law). Surprisingly, the general granted her an audience. She then made him a startling proposal – if he spared both herself and Leamaneh Castle, historic strong-hold of the O'Briens, she would marry any man in his army, thus making her new husband (with her) master of the O'Brien lands. Intrigued by the offer, Ireton agreed and posted a notice to that effect amongst his troops. Most English soldiers thought that it was a joke but a lowly bugler, John Cooper, came forward. Shortly after, in 1651, Ireton died at Limerick from a plague that was sweeping the city and the rumourmongers attributed his demise to witchcraft – a spell laid on him by Máire Rua during his audience with her. By this time she was already married to Cooper and the bugler was now, in effect, legally the Lord of Leamaneh.

It is said that her new husband was both a gambler and a wast-rel and soon had lost much of the family fortune. Despite this, Máire Rua herself continued to live in reasonable comfort – although not always at Leamaneh but in a number of smaller O'Brien castles around the countryside. How she managed to do this is unclear but she seems to have been able to maintain a relatively luxurious lifestyle for about the next ten or twelve years. This, once again, fuelled allegations of her witchcraft.

There are conflicting accounts of what actually happened to John Cooper – some say that, after 'a decent period', he and Máire Rua separated and he was given a small portion of the remaining O'Brien fortune which he frittered away, eventually dying in poverty; others say that he fell from one of the windows in Leamaneh Castle and broke his neck. Máire, however, continued as a considerable O'Brien figure, retaining at least the vestiges of her former wealth and power. But the death of Cromwell and the restoration of the king — Charles II — were soon to create problems for her. The new regime did not take kindly to her and accused her of latterly supporting the Cromwellians in Ireland and formerly of murdering English settlers. In the end, it fell to the king himself to grant her a royal pardon, which he did in 1664. However, in return, she had to give up Leamaneh and agree to a number of restrictions.

So she left her former stronghold, extremely reluctantly, and went to live in Dromoland Castle, County Clare. Even there, whispers of witchcraft still pursued her and it was suggested that she might be seeking to harm King Charles by foul arts. The allegations came to nothing and her son, Donough O'Brien, was created a baron by Charles's brother, James II, allowing Dromoland to become an official O'Brien seat. It was here that Máire died peacefully in 1686.

Legends about her persisted long after her death. She had allegedly been seen, as a ghost, around some ancient O'Brien castles and, like the Earl Fitzgerald, it was said that she would carry away those she met into the afterlife. One local person maintains that on her father's farm lie the ruins of an old O'Brien castle which local people are afraid to go near after dark for fear 'the witch woman' (Máire Rua) would capture them. It seems that even today, so many centuries later, Red Mary O'Brien is not quite forgotten.

* * *

The various tales of witchcraft attributed to the Fitzgeralds and the O'Briens were probably little more than propaganda put about by their enemies. As the former Gaelic aristocracy — particularly those that had opposed English settlement — began to fade away both in status and power, there seems to have been something of an effort to portray them in a less than favourable light. In this respect, spreading rumours of witchcraft or wizardry had an obvious purpose.

Although such accusations had more or less died out in Ireland with the eighteenth-century Islandmagee case (see chapter three), at around the beginning of the nineteenth century a curious allegation of witchcraft was brought in the north of the country, when a case appeared at the Spring Assizes in Carrickfergus in March 1808.

Much of our information about this case comes from *The Belfast News-Letter* for August 1807 and concerns Mary Butters, the celebrated 'witch of Carnmoney'. The incident brought before the court began at the house of a tailor, Alexander Montgomery, who lived quite close to Carnmoney Meeting House. Like Islandmagee, the village of Carnmoney was largely a Presbyterian community but there was also an undercurrent of superstition running through the place.

Alexander Montgomery had one cow on which he and his

family depended. The animal continued to give milk but the milk which it gave would not churn nor would it make butter or cream. Montgomery's wife had a superstitious turn of mind and became convinced that the cow had been bewitched by person or persons unknown. She tried several charms in order to lift the 'enchantment' but without success. After making some enquiries throughout the locality, she heard of a woman named Mary Butters, who lived between Carnmoney and Carrickfergus and who allegedly had the power to 'cure' afflicted cattle and to restore milk. Both Mrs Montgomery and her husband went to see this woman and brought her back with them to the house, hoping that she would cure the cow. The woman examined the beast and then with earnest consideration told Montgomery that unknown magicians had indeed bewitched it but that she could probably lift the spell.

She then told Alexander Montgomery and a young man named Carnaghan to go and stand in the cattle byre, turn their waistcoats inside out and to remain there until she sent for them. They were to stand close to the head of the affected cow but they were not to touch her. Montgomery's wife, son and an old woman called Margaret Lee were to remain in the house with her. When the men had gone, Mary Butters locked and sealed the door and prepared her antidote.

Taking a large pot which she put on the crook above the fire, she filled it with water and when it was boiling, she added 'certain noxious substances' (one of which was thought to have been sulphur), milk, needles, pins and crooked nails.

This, she said, was to 'draw down' the witch that had blighted them. Over the pot, she began to recite her spells.

Outside in the cowshed, Alexander Montgomery and his young companion waited. Having received no summons to the house, they became concerned as the hours went by. At last Montgomery decided to go back to the house and see what was happening. He knocked on the locked door and, receiving no response, went round to a side window and looked in. There, to his horror, he saw the four of them stretched out on the floor as if dead. Calling to the boy, he immediately broke down the door and burst into the room, being almost overcome by an extremely strong smell of sulphur. Reaching the four bodies, he found that his wife and son were actually dead and that Mary Butters and Margaret Lee were nearly so. Before she could be revived, Margaret Lee expired but helpers were able to drag Mary Butters out onto a dungheap where she was revived by means of a few hearty kicks to the ribs. The room in which they had been fairly reeked of sulphur and it was agreed that the three fatalities had been caused by suffocation. The door had been locked and all holes and apertures had been sealed to prevent 'evil spirits' from entering. A mixture of sweet milk and water had been heated to boiling point over the fire to which had been added three rows of new pins, three packages of needles and three crooked nails. This was considered, throughout the locality, as an infallible method of 'banishing witches' and was used by a 'conjurer' in Newtowards for that purpose as late as 1871/72. Mary Butters further seems to have added some ingredients of her own, such as herbs and sulphur — the latter causing the deaths of her unfortunate clients.

At an inquest held at Carnmoney village on 19 August 1807, it was decided that the deaths of the two Montgomerys and of Margaret Lee had been caused by Mary Butters' pretence at witchcraft, claiming that she could cure the sick cow. She was, therefore, returned for trial at the Spring Assizes. In her defence, the 'witch of Carnmoney' stated that indeed the 'anti-bewitchment' was commencing to work but that unknown sorcerers had sent a spirit, in the guise of a huge black-skinned man carrying a club, to halt the proceedings and it was this demon that had killed the victims and knocked herself unconscious. Her story was, of course, dismissed. Nevertheless, the court took the view that the whole sorry affair had been 'accidental death' caused by 'gross superstition and credulousness' and Mary Butters was discharged by proclamation. In spite of this, she attained some local notoriety as a witch and a racy ballad concerning the incident and poking fun both at the witch and at those who believed in witchcraft was penned anonymously in what was termed 'Braid Scots' (a dialect used by the Presbyterians of the area) by some waggish bard. The following is an excerpt:

'For who can read their mystic matters,
  Or tell if sweethearts be true.
The folks a' run tae Mary Butters,

To tell what thief a horse did steal,

In this she was a mere pretender,

An' has nae art to raise the De'il [Devil].

Like that auld wife, the Witch of Endor.

If Mary Butters be a witch

Why but the people all should no it,

An' if she can the muses touch,

I'm sure she'll soon descry the poet'.

The unknown rhymer, of course, ensured that the 'witch of Carnmoney' would live on in folk tradition for years to come. But the nature of the doggerel shows how public perception of witches, and those who traded with them, was changing. No longer were they people to be feared and shunned, rather they were figures of mockery and fun.

Today the popular vision of the witch has changed even further – they are now almost mythical creatures that appear around Hallowe'en or in Disney cartoons, more geared towards children than adults. Hags with black cats and broomsticks, they are not to be taken all that seriously – at least on the surface. But perhaps locked away in some remote corner of the mind there is still the age-old wariness of the crone, the woman who is rumoured to be able to 'do things'. These people may still be treated with respect and deference – just in case. The dark shadow of the sorceress may not have completely disappeared.

Other books from The O'Brien Press

A HAUNTED LAND
Ireland's Ghosts
Bob Curran

A chilling collection of stories of supernatural occurrences gathered from all
around Ireland. Curran has written a
haunting portrayal of a land and a people
steeped in the lore of death and the afterlife.

Paperback €9.95/STG£6.99

LEGENDARY IRELAND
A Journey through Celtic Places and Myths
Eithne Massey

A journey through the places and legends
of Celtic Ireland - a land of warriors,
queens, gods and goddesses. It visits
twenty eight richly atmospheric sites and
tells their mythological stories, featuring
the heroic characters of Celtic lore, such as
Cú Chulainn, Oisín, Queen Maeve, Diar-
muid and Gráinne. Beautifully illlustrated with haunting
photographs and elegant engravings.

Hardback €24.95/STG£17.99

CELTIC WAY OF LIFE
Curriculum Development Unit
Illus. Josip Lizatovic (plus photos)

How the Celts lived in ancient Ireland- their houses, food, weapons, modes of transport, social structures, beliefs and their pagan festivals and rituals. A concise, accessible introduction to a fascinating period in Ireland's history .

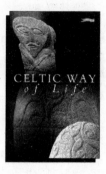

Paperback €7.61/STG£5.99

Send for our full-colour catalogue

ORDER FORM

Please send me the books as marked.

I enclose cheque/postal order for € . . . .

(Please include €2.50 P&P per title)

OR please charge my credit card ☐ Access/Mastercard ☐ Visa

Card Number _ _ _ _   _ _ _ _   _ _ _ _   _ _ _ _

Expiry Date _ _ / _ _

Name. . . . . Tel . . . .

Address . . . .

. . . .

Please send orders to: THE O'BRIEN PRESS, 20 Victoria Road, Dublin 6, Ireland.

Tel: +353 1 4923333; Fax: +353 1 4922777; E-mail: books@obrien.ie

Website: www.obrien.ie
Please note: prices are subject to change without notice